The Perfect Choral Workbook

Tools to Organize Your Choral Program

By Timothy Seelig

Book design by Shawn Northcutt

Copying Is Illegal

ISBN 978-1-59235-199-2

Shawnee Press, Inc. §
1107 17th Avenue South • Nashville, TN 37212

Table of Contents

Acknowledgements

No one who ever wrote or compiled a book did so completely on their own. Certainly this book could never have been compiled by one person. In fact, it is the cumulative result of many, many people who have contributed to the last 35 years of my musical career. I thank you all for the part you have played and your invaluable contribution.

Most recently, however, I have had very specific assistance from some great friends and wonderful colleagues. They, in turn, have gleaned their knowledge from a host of other extraordinary people.

Those I wish to thank include:

Pam Elrod, head of choral studies at Southern Methodist University where I teach. Pam had the great honor of studying with, and therefore we thank by proxy, Robert Shaw, Robert Bode, Whitman College; and Bill Thomas, Furman University.

Lynn Brinckmeyer, choral and music education faculty at Texas State University and president of Music Educators National Conference.

Natalie Waters, choral music educator, Highland Park High School, Dallas, Texas.

Gary Holt, attorney and conductor of the Gay Men's Chorus of San Diego, California.

Hugh Davies, musician, singer and President of ACFEA worldwide concert promotion company.

Bruce Wynne Jones and Damien Gough, extraordinary public relations and advertising gurus from Brand-Agent, Dallas, Texas.

James Jordan, who needs no description (and who defies it anyway).

Juanelle Teague, author, speaker, charismatic leader; developer of "Specialize or Die" and People, Plus, Inc.

My trusty proofreaders: Kenn, Mark, Robert, and Gary. It's the third book for all of you. I promise the next will be the "tell all" life story – a much easier read.

All of the wonderful people at Shawnee Press who keep me on task, from President, Mark Cabaniss right on "up" the line to Greg, Anissa, Krista, and all of the great people there.

Shawn Northcutt, for making all of the products with my name on them look so good.

And, of course, my family for being so patient with me. We choral conductor/musicians are not the easiest people on earth to get along with – so I hear. Hard to imagine, but I'll take their word for it!

Foreword

It all began a long, long time ago as I spent my toddler years occupying myself while my mother took voice lessons, vocal coachings, taught voice lessons herself, performed all over the world, and dragged me with her as she pursued what turned out to be a wonderful singing and teaching career.

Other than the exquisite music she made with her glorious contralto voice, what resonated with me was her absolute love and passion for the medium of the voice and her deep belief that lives and minds could be changed through the communion between performer and listener. It was never enough just to perform the notes on the page; it was all about connection through music. It was a lesson I am so grateful to have learned at her feet.

Even though I never intended to, I ended up following in my Mother's footsteps, taking voice lessons, vocal coachings, taught voice, traveled across the globe plying my own musical trade. The only difference was that somewhere along the way, I veered from the solo career, opting instead to stand in front of a bunch of singers, with my back to the audience, happily being the conduit through which others raised their voices in communication with all who would listen. I learned that while I absolutely loved facing an audience, I loved even more facing the singers who would move the audience through me.

A few years ago, after I had been singing and conducting for only 30 years, Greg Gilpin asked if I would write a book about warming up the voice for choral singing. After some thought and encouragement, I said I would try.

Those 30 years of professional singing, teaching and conducting resulted in the first book and subsequent DVD, "The Perfect Blend." The humorous, logical, step-by-step approach to choral warm-ups as they relate to eating a fine five-course meal, apparently struck a chord with folks out there.

Thus followed a sequel about rehearsal technique. After 20 years of conducting the same chorus, in addition to numerous others along the way, it was assumed by the publishers that I might know a little about how to plan rehearsals and motivate singers. Thus, the book and DVD, "The Perfect Rehearsal," told through the analogy of travel – another love of mine.

Finally (he says emphatically), the third in the trilogy has arrived and is in your hands. You know, being a choir director is HARD! They didn't tell us that in school. It takes a huge amount of organization if you are to be successful. Thus, the final book in this series, "The Perfect Choral Workbook," includes forms and lists that will help you in your work and entertain you along the way.

All I can say at this point is that I am **perfectly** thrilled that so many people have benefited from my having written down some of the joys of my career. I hope you enjoy them as well.

Introduction

With over 35 years as a choral conductor under my proverbial belt, I realized that 50 percent of what I had accomplished had been by accident. The other 50 percent was the result of being really organized! One of my "comfort zones" was constantly making checklists and filling out forms.

In the Myers Briggs Personality Profile, the last letter of the four words that describe each of us is either "P" for Perceiver or "J" for Judger. All that really means is that if you are a "P," you prefer to float through life, taking it as it comes. If you are a "J," you are a list maker, organizing yourself and everyone around you. Boy, am I a "J." This book is for the "Ps" and the "Js."

For you fellow "Js," this book is going to be comforting and reassuring. You are going to look at these lists and forms and simply think, "Duh!". For you "Ps" however, this book may be a revelation. You may have moments where you say, "Why didn't I think of that?" In many cases, it was my colleagues who helped me fill in the blanks where my experience had not allowed me the opportunity. For those of you who are "Ps," this book may be a little irritating. But please bear with me. It will be worth it in the end.

The book is organized in the following way:

- An explanation of the issue at hand.
- A sample of the form. Some of them are partially filled out as an example.
- The full form is on the CD in the back of the book for you to use, copy, tweak, etc.

You may already have a form that you use for an exact purpose, but in looking at these, you may decide there is a better or different way, or something to add to your existing one.

The best advice I can give anyone picking up this book is to "keep reading." You may begin it and think it is so obvious you wonder why you forked out the big bucks for such a tool. But if you will keep going and trust the process, you will find some amazing things herein. As I began to gather a lifetime of organizational tools, I was amazed at some of the things I had forgotten. Then I gathered the same from colleagues around the country in areas that were not automatic to me – travel, branding, public school education, etc.

When I say trust the process, I can remind you of how you do that with your own singers. For example, when you pass out that song you heard over the summer break and absolutely fell in love with when the room full of choir directors sang it. Your singers then attempt to sight-read it. They immediately think you have lost your grip on reality. How could you have thought this would ever be perceived as "music" by the listeners? They politely resist.

You exhort them to; trust the process; be patient; learn the notes; read the words; fix the rhythms; consider the relationship of the text and the music; don't just listen to their own part, but wait until it all comes together. Week by week, the tables gradually turn and the naysayers are actually in the minority. Then the performance: the audience loves it and the singers, whose memories are shorter than your own, proclaim that it was their favorite piece the entire time!

In the same way, trust the process in reading this book. Do the exercises. Read the lists. Fill out the forms. And remember to write me when something really clicks for you! There will be parts of the book that are just for you. There are other parts that are for your singers. There are still others that relate to your audience. I look forward to hearing from you and adding your input to the website **www.choralquest.com** when you send it my way!

So, now that you know where we are going, let's get started and don't forget to look for

B.o.B.!

Whenever a form is included on the enclosed CD, you will see our little friend "B.o.B" (as in Back of Book).

List of "B.o.B"s
(in order of appearance)

Chapter 1: Looking Back

Only by knowing how you got where you are, can you move forward and plan successfully. In addition, a look back is always a healthy thing. It is also a great tool in helping others – our students – know how they can move forward in their own lives.

When I look back, one of my favorite topics is "Things they forgot to teach or were afraid we would find out!"

Each step of the way, we take stock of the things that have brought us to this point. For many of us, regardless of how much "schoolin'" we had, it was only when we actually began doing what we do, that we got a clue as to what it actually entailed. Looking back, it is a good thing that we don't know it all up front. Funny thing about that wisdom part of life. This is something that can only be learned with age.

Now don't get me wrong, our music education was invaluable. However, we do tend to become insulated and isolated in the university setting. Many of the things that are important in the higher education setting are not mirrored outside of that sequestered environment. What is taught and works inside that "bubble" is not always what works outside of it. The real world always has lessons that simply can't be taught; they simply have to be experienced.

On the other hand, I do sometimes wish my colleagues in higher education had more "real world" experience. It would be invaluable. Sometimes, I find that it is the very things we go to school to learn that are systematically beaten out of us. We learn musicianship instead of musicality. We learn counterpoint instead of communication. We learn to crush our creative spirit to fit inside the box prescribed by our professors. That having being said, here are some of the things they didn't tell us, or certainly didn't tell me:

Things They Didn't To Teach You

- You'll probably lose your voice the first year you teach - and every fall thereafter.
- You won't know one song you can actually use the first day you meet and hear your first choir.
- Your schedule isn't going to get easier once you graduate - it gets worse.
- There are no "famous" singers who are also "famous" conductors. These two are difficult career bedfellows.
- Straight tone is a vocal fault (I always throw that one in just for fun).
- You will be competing for audience members and entertainment dollars.
- You can kill a concert by allowing the audience to applaud after every song (or you talking).
- You don't have to beat every beat of every piece. Learn the term "Negate."
- Music is a means to an end, not the end itself.
- If you have done your job, your singers don't need you nearly as much as you would like to think they do.
- It's not all about you. Ouch!
- You trained to be a conductor. There were no classes in how to be a fundraiser, counselor, pastor, cheerleader, therapist, baby-sitter, accountant, referee, travel agent, or bouncer.
- It's OK for a "legitimate" choir to move, use theatrical enhancements, props, and even costumes, when appropriate.
- Choral performances can actually be fun.
- Less is more. You are better off to perform a one-hour concert really well than a two-hour concert that is just OK.

Who Am I?

Are we just robots? Does someone teach us the "moves" and then along the way we simply press "play" and off we go? Are we just clones of our own choral directors and mentors? Are we afraid to be unique? Are we afraid to question?

Are we doing this job because someone told us we should do it? Are we doing it because we don't know what else to do?

The present is always a good time to delve deep inside and look at what makes us tick – what makes us do what we do. This is when we need to look at our core values.

Core values make up your belief system and make you unique. It is also these values from which you derive the energy you need for your life's work. To be successful, you need to not only know, but prioritize your core values. The top five values will provide you with the passion you need to do your job, do it well, and fuel your activities.

Without knowing exactly what your own core values are, you are at the mercy of others placing theirs upon you. This will never work. You will never be happy or successful in what you do as long as you are living on someone else's value system.

One of the most difficult things in establishing your own core values is honesty. Some of them may sound negative, but in reality, they are simply honest.

This first assignment is to select the ten values of greatest concern to you. Do not answer based on what others might list for you or what you think others might think, should they see your answers!

After you have selected your top 10, go back and rank them 1–10, with "1" being the highest.

Then, write down your top five core values because these are, indeed, your true internal motivators. If you are honest, you may be surprised.

Core Values

Check your top 10 Core Values. Then prioritize them.

Value	*Priority*	*Rank*
Financial Security	✔	2
Respect for Others	✔	7
Recognition		
Personal Freedom/Independence	✔	8
Family Cohesiveness	✔	9
Spirituality/Faith		
Organized Environment		
Structured Routine		
Punctuality	✔	6
Efficient Use of Time		
Personal Solitude		
Creativity	✔	1
Influence over Others		
Knowledge		
To Be Appreciated		
Good Health	✔	5
Challenges		
Excitement/Adventure	✔	10
Competition		
Productivity		
Inner Peace		
Experience Love and Affection		
Successful Relationships	✔	4
Service to Others	✔	3
Wisdom		

How Did I Get Here?

This next exercise is one of the most important and useful tools I have ever seen or done. It was developed by life coach extraordinaire, Juanelle Teague. I certainly wish I had known about it much earlier in my life. It is a document that you can work on for a long time and will want to keep for the rest of your life.

The concept is fairly simple and yet daunting at the same time. It involves creating a list of one significant memory/experience for each year you have been alive. When I was first presented with this idea, I thought to myself, "I can hardly remember what I did last year, much less 20 or 30 years ago." Then, because I was paying a significant amount of money for someone to walk me through this process, I sat down and started. Here's how:

Find some time in a comfortable setting. Start with the obvious – not just dates, times, places – but the obvious and momentous occurrences in your life. From these, you will begin to be able to fill in the blanks – a year before or a year after.

WARNING: the memories will begin to flow. You may write down only one per year. Select the most significant one that in some way changed you or changed the course of your life. There will be many years in which you would like to write a complete list of things that may have occurred. But, to make the process work most effectively, you need to select just one per year. This is the only way to create a "big picture" look at your entire life. Patterns will emerge. You will begin to see the junctures at which your life took various turns.

Juanelle suggests that each of us will find six turning points once the entire form is filled out for your entire life!

The first three occur during your social/educational years of development. They involve the people and events that surrounded you from birth through college. These usually occur at the ages of 3 or 4, 10–13 and 14–24.

The second set of three happens during your more "mature" years of life and revolves around personal relationships and career.

Life Highlights

The turning points may have been positive or negative. But the most important thing about each of them is that they taught you life lessons and eventually helped form the person you are today. This can be taken from a purely personal standpoint, or from the standpoint of your musical life. Sometimes, they are inextricable.

There are so many incredible outcomes from this exercise: not only for you, but for those around you – friends, family, coworkers, students. They will all benefit from you taking the time to do this. I can't encourage you enough to do this – for yourself, if for no one else.

Here is a sample.

Life Highlights

Age	Year	Event	People Involved	Environment	Feelings
0					
1					
2					
3					
4	1955	Romper Room	Mother	TV Studio	Failure
5	1956	Voice Lessons	Mother	Home	Curiosity
6	1957	Kindergarten	Teacher	School	Fun!
7	1958	Move	Family/Friends	New Town	Insecure
8	1959	Move	Teacher/Friends	New School	Comfortable
9	1960	Art	Teacher/Family	Home	Hurt
10	1961	Talent Show	Friends/Family	Public Performance	Accomplishment
11	1962	Football	Bobby/Scott	Team	Really BAD!
12	1963	Playing Bass	Teacher	Orchestr	New Musica
13	1964	pping	Jewish	Neiman	Paridig
14	196	der		9	
15	1				

Respect for ~
Family Cohesiveness
Spirituality Faith
Punctuality
Creativity
Good Health
Challenges
Successful Relationship
Service to Others
Inner Peace

Is My Job?

...eeds an up-to-date job description. Period.
...erlook. In most cases, no one is going to do

...ssuming that because everything is going
...begin our jobs with a current description
...r the years, things change. Duties are
...ore duties are added. We are filling in
...knows all of the various things we do
...less we document it! (Don't you just
...noral director is a "cushy" job or even

...sually new to the group, and asks,
...r sometimes it may be "Why is he/

...on or persons who hired us are no longer in the picture.
...this was a verbal agreement when I took the job," will not suffice.
...won't work to say, "This is the way I have always done it." You need to
have an updated job description for your protection, if for no other reason.

My suggestion is that you put at least one very important item on your yearly "To
Do" list: **Update Job Description**.

Completing the task includes getting the appropriate people in positions of
authority to sign off on it. This should be something you request every single year.
The new job description will be attached to your annual evaluation and placed in
your personnel file, for your protection, as well as that of your employer.

It should also include the goals that you have set for the next year on the job. The
simple act of writing down everything you do will enlighten and even surprise
you and definitely anyone else with whom you share it.

JOB DESCRIPTION (Sample)
Conductor

Date: _____

A. Conductor/Artistic Director Responsibilities

The Conductor's responsibilities are primarily musical. He/she should be able to plan and direct all of the music in a given season: rehearsals, performances, recordings, tours. The Artistic Director should maintain a visible image in the city and across the country. The general direction of the chorus will depend on the vision of this position and it is crucial that the organization support the musical/artistic vision. The position includes artistic representation of the chorus, public image, and unity of purpose/ vision for the membership.

B. Principal Duties

1. Musical Direction

A major portion of this involves research into repertoire for the chorus in order to stay on the cutting edge musically while satisfying the desires of the patrons. Then comes the selection and preparation of the repertoire for the chorus and its subgroups. This may also involve meeting with composers and arrangers. This selection and preparation is for all concerts in a given season, recordings and tours. The final step includes the study of scores, preparation and planning of rehearsals, concert order, timing, pacing, etc.

2. Performances and Rehearsals

The conductor is responsible for all performances and rehearsals.

3. Administration of Performance-Related Activities

These duties include oversight and coordination of all details for each rehearsal and performance: venue, sound, lights, soloists, instrumentalists, dancers, choreographers, directors, etc. The administration of the artistic product includes production of e-notes every week, and providing input into production of promotion materials and advertising as requested.

4. Administration of the Artistic/Production Staff

The Artistic Director is the direct supervisor of the artistic staff, which may include both full-time and part-time employees. The coordination of their duties is crucial to the ongoing artistic quality of the organization. This includes all personnel issues, from time management to salary negotiations.

5. Intra-Chorus Development

Building rapport and esprit de corps is crucial. The Conductor should be available to the membership when they have needs or concerns. It is important to be responsive to productivity tools, provide positive musical and personal feedback to the membership, and participate in proactive development of family enhancement.

6. Coordinate/Conduct Subgroups

The coordination includes guidance of directors, repertoire, accompanists, rehearsal space and performance venues, times, places and ensuring the quality of performance. The Artistic Director may conduct one or more of the *subgroups*.

7. Public Image

The Conductor is the face of the organization.

8. Vision for the Future

The Conductor works with various groups as specified to provide vision and vehicles for continued growth.

9. Business and Administrative Operations

The Conductor will work with the administration as necessary and appropriate in order to coordinate artistic operations with the business and administrative operations.

C. Reporting and Relationships

1. **Reports Directly to:** Board Chair/Principal

2. **Works With:** President/Executive Director

3. **Directly Supervises:** Artistic/Production Staff

Goals are attached for upcoming year or season.

How Am I Doing?

Later on in the book and on the CD are some forms that can be used by others to evaluate you, your conducting, and your management of a choral program. For now, we are still in the self-evaluation phase. This form is a tool I have used for many years to give an overall sense of where a choral educator stands. It is something I think we should examine each year to see where we might spend our "continuing education" to its best effect. Keep this simple form handy, and fill it out every year. Use these broad rankings for your self-evaluation at the beginning and end of each year that you are in a choral position.

We all like to work on our strengths and we gravitate toward workshops and continuing education opportunities that are within our comfort zone. Human nature is to shy away from areas in which we do not excel or with which we are not automatically comfortable. This evaluation may help you identify some of those weaker areas and challenge you to seek to improve on those rather than continue to improve the areas where you are already doing a great job.

For example, if you get the same comments from judges, adjudicators or audience members year after year, you may be able to diagnose the problems, but you are not able to prescribe how to fix those problems. If you ask one of your singers to lead the warm-ups, including explanations of why they are doing them, and they are unable to do it at the drop of a hat, you are probably teaching clones, not concepts!

Such self-improvement is an area in which we need to seek help outside our current circle of friends, teachers, mentors, etc. They know us too well. Gather some colleagues together and work through this simple exercise in a nonthreatening group. You'll be surprised what everyone is willing to share and what you will learn.

This is also a tool that can be used for your students as they begin to think about careers in music or in determining areas where they might need to put some energy and focus.

Self-Examination For Choral Conductors

Seven Pillars of Artistic Success

These are the things upon which your career as a musician is built. Rank yourself 1 – 5 on the following skills. 1 is the lowest, 5 is the highest.

1. **Talent** 1 2 3 4 5
   (innate ability)
2. **Vocal/Choral Technique** 1 2 3 4 5
   (how you have improved your natural talent)
3. **Musicianship** 1 2 3 4 5
   (knowledge of the vocal instrument)
4. **Artistic Imagination** 1 2 3 4 5
   (making music your own)
5. **Objectivity** 1 2 3 4 5
   (Step back and evaluate.)
6. **Perseverance** 1 2 3 4 5
   (Could you do anything else and be happy?)
7. **Business Acumen** 1 2 3 4 5
   (Excel spreadsheets?)

Total _____

Seven is the lowest and thirty-five is the highest. Upon completion, you should have a good idea of where areas of improvement lie.

Five Principles for Successful Conducting/Teaching

These are things upon which your career as a conductor/teacher is built. Rank yourself 1 – 5 on the following skills. 1 is the lowest, 5 is the highest.

1. **Conductor/Singer Rapport** 1 2 3 4 5
   (Doggone it! ... they like me.)
2. **Diagnosis and Prescription** 1 2 3 4 5
   (Can you fix the problems?)
3. **Specificity of Language** 1 2 3 4 5
   (Are you teaching concepts not clones?)
4. **Efficient Use of Time** 1 2 3 4 5
   (Do you plan your rehearsals well?)
5. **Measurable Results** 1 2 3 4 5
   (Do you achieve your goals?)

Total _____

Add up your scores. If you gave yourself a five, you might consider seeking other vocational opportunities or, at the very least, therapy. If you gave yourself a twenty-five, you should probably be teaching this session.

Who Is My Chorus?

It doesn't matter what kind of chorus you conduct – school, church, community, symphony, or the phone company retiree choir – each one has its own unique personality. Certainly choirs of similar genres have many things in common, but just as the individual singers in your group, the collective has its own characteristics as well.

How do we discover our very own niche in the community? How do we set ourselves apart – in a good way – from the other choruses in our area? How do we compete with other activities that draw people to them?

All too often our choirs take on our personalities. This is not a bad thing. In fact, it can mean that you are not just a robot, but are actually providing visionary leadership for your group. This is invaluable. Regardless of what kind of chorus you conduct – and chances are you conduct more than one – making discoveries about your chorus is a fantastic exercise. One of the most important ways to do that is with some sort of 360-degree **"branding"** exercise for the chorus, or each of your choruses. This can best be done by you and a small group of people who are involved on different levels.

The 360-degree concept is one that includes your boss, a selection of peers, subordinates, and customers or stakeholders (for us, that would be audience). Having someone who is not intimately involved, but perhaps has just a passing knowledge of your group, is also worthwhile. This will help you be more objective about the perceptions of who you are and what you are doing outside of your immediate circle.

There are many sophisticated tools available – and many companies who will be happy to charge you a great deal of money to do this for you. But much of the work has to be done by you anyway! The real mastery comes in the synthesis of the information and then crafting that into a form that is useful to your group.

There is a difference in a mission statement and a vision statement. Every group should have one of each. Your mission statement is most often something you use for the public: it states who you are and what you do. The vision statement is used internally: it states who you want to be or hope to be. These are incredibly useful tools.

About ten years ago, the Turtle Creek Chorale hired a firm to do just such a branding exercise and develop a new tag line for the group. They asked people who were not in the chorus what one thing came to mind about the Chorale. The consensus? The sound!

Had they asked me or the singers, we would probably have thought of many other things that were important to us such as the family feel created within the group, the outreach we did in the community, etc. But at that time, the public relations firm felt that most people outside the organization equated who we were with the sound we made. Thus, the tag line they developed was "Like No Other Sound On Earth." We used it for many years. It was positive and at the same time did not diminish anyone else in the field.

The **"Creative Brief"** that follows is from one of the finest advertising firms with whom I have ever had the opportunity to work, Brand-Agent. I have worked with them twice in the last year and have been amazed at their sensitivity and intuitiveness. This brief is just one of the tools they use in ascertaining who an organization is and how best to get to the core of the issues and the "personality" of a group. The actual Creative Brief they use is much more complex than the one here. This has been streamlined to focus on a choral group.

Create a small group of people from inside and outside your organization – somewhere between five and ten. Send the brief to them and ask everyone to fill it out. Set a deadline for getting the forms returned (to you or someone who really likes to tabulate such things!). Then meet to go over the results with the entire group so everyone has a chance for feedback. With no names attached, take each question one at a time and look at everyone's comments. You will be absolutely amazed at what you learn.

This exercise will give you an idea of the past, present, and future of your organization. You may be shocked with some of the perceptions and certainly with the wide variety of answers. From this exercise, you will learn not only what people think of the organization, but certainly some of the areas of concern that need refining.

CREATIVE BRIEF

Date: _____

Name of Chorus/Organization:

Overview

Step back and consider the big picture. This is the 30,000-foot view. What challenges do you face? Why is this assignment important? What is the competitive landscape? What are recent trends in the field (e.g., more audience-friendly production value in choral concerts)?

Current Personality and Positioning

Describe the personality (brand) and how it is currently positioned. How do stockholders or potential stockholders describe your chorus? What is the unique selling proposition? What is the benefit and reason to believe?

Objectives (Desired Outcome)

Outline the objectives of the assignment and/or the brand. What are the overall marketing objectives? How do we make more of an impact on our community? How do we reach a larger audience for our concerts?

Strategies

Include specific strategies that will help achieve the objectives.
For example, defining the mission and goals of the chorus.

Target Audience

Describe the various audiences the project is intended to reach. This should include demographics and also internal audiences, as well as impact on internal stockholders. This would be chorus members, family, friends, and the entire world!

Look / Feel / Mood / Desired Voice / Tone

Describe the way in which the communication should be presented (fun, energetic, supportive, creative, nurturing, appeal to teens, tweens, seniors, wholesome, sophisticated, etc.).

Key Product and Attributes

Include information on the product itself that may be helpful to know during the creative development process. This can be the historical perspective of the group and should include what you do, such as sing concerts, community service, tours, recordings, etc.

Support of the Project / Exercise

Is this part of an existing or new campaign? Who cares about your chorus and who will help?

Competition

List the competitors. What sets your brand apart? For example, your competition is whatever is going on in your city on the night of a concert! Who else in town is providing the same services?

Measure of Success

Will data be gathered and measured? Surveys?

Branding Team

Identify which team members will be assigned to the project.

Communication Priorities

State the call to action. What do you wish to accomplish with this exercise? For example, focus your efforts and increase audience.

Approval

Who needs to be included? Principal, President, Chair of the Board?

Chapter 2: Looking Ahead

We all get wrapped up in the "daily days" of our lives; they just seem to come with such regularity! It is all too easy to get in a rut and be a cog in the manufacturing of widgets. We have "cookie-cutter" days, "cookie-cutter" concerts, "cookie-cutter" choral programs, and turn out "cookie-cutter" singers and students. How do we stop the insanity and get off the proverbial merry-go-round?

Sometimes it isn't even that we spend too much time and energy focused on the "daily days," but rather the past. How many of your colleagues continually discuss the good old days and their past triumphs? How many of them drone on and on about the ruination of their glorious choral programs at the hands of insensitive or unappreciative administrators, block scheduling, lack of funding, the loss of an assistant or accompanist or the advent of Rap music?

My hope is that you have taken several really important steps. You have taken some time to look back at what has brought you to this point. You have looked inside at the person you have become. You have also taken the time to look at "Who am I?" and "Who is my chorus?". If you have done all of this, then you've finished your vegetables and can have dessert.

There are many authors who suggest to readers to simply "follow the money." Well, that won't work for us. We decided long ago to "follow our passion" instead. Hopefully, we can make a living at it at the same time.

But that won't happen without a willingness to make a plan. And it won't happen without creating **balance** in your life, this being one of the life skills that has been woefully skipped over in our education process. We represent some of the most unbalanced professions imaginable. Let's look at what it would take to regain or discover some healthy balance.

Six Principals of Balance

There are six **Principals of Balance** for your life. All too often, we focus on one or two to the detriment of the others. What if we gave equal energy to each? How would our lives change for the better? Here are some questions to ask yourself.

1. Physical. Am I in good health? Do I present a good role model for the singers I conduct and mentor? Am I in good vocal health?

2. Mental. Am I taking care of my own emotional needs? Have I created balance in my own life? Do I have appropriate input and assistance to stay focused and on track mentally?

3. Spiritual. Do I know how to take care of me? Do I take time and devote the energy necessary to develop a higher consciousness and a deeper sense of the world in which I live? Am I doing anything to make the world a better place?

4. Relationships. Have I given appropriate time and energy to the people who are most important in my life and who will be with me year after year? What have I done specifically to nurture the people closest to me?

5. Financial. Am I taking care of my financial needs? Have I taken care of those around me lest something happens to me?

6. Career. Am I continuing to develop in the areas in which I know I am weakest? Am I just hanging on because I don't know what else to do and someone told me I would be good at it? What can I do to broaden my scope of interests and, at the same time, deepen my knowledge of what I am currently doing?

One of the most difficult challenges in life is to achieve balance. Often, we do not have healthy role models, especially in the musical world. As stated, a musical career is a difficult path and one that most often includes multiple jobs to make ends meet. The above six principals become more important with every year we ply our craft as musicians.

Principals of Balance

Goals

5-10 Years

What are some of my long-range goals for the future?

Musical   _____
Physical   _____
Mental   _____
Spiritual   _____
Relationships   _____
Financial   _____
Career   _____

3-5 Years

What can I accomplish in the next few years to set the tone for the future?

Musical   _____
Physical   _____
Mental   _____
Spiritual   _____
Relationships   _____
Financial   _____
Career   _____

This Year

What can I accomplish this year for myself and my career?

Musical   _____
Physical   _____
Mental   _____
Spiritual   _____
Relationships   _____
Financial   _____
Career   _____

Musical Maps

Why would you need maps as a conductor? Well, as with any trip, you begin with the "big picture" map first. This is the one that has only the starting point and the destination. From there, you begin to focus on the details in descending order. The next map would include points of interest or importance along the way. Finally, you would end with a very detailed map of the actual destination - including things such as where a museum might be, or where you want to eat dinner, or even as detailed as how to get from the lobby of the hotel to your room! As conductors, we do the same thing. **We need maps!**

We start with what the next 3–5 years will look like: seasons, concerts, tours, recordings. Next we whittle that down to a map of what the next year or season will look like: how do the concerts ebb and flow and provide a full gamut of experiences for singers and audience. Then, we need a map of what each concert will look like. This includes the repertoire, possible guest artists, accompaniment, highs, lows – and possible detours. It also includes how to incorporate TLC! Finally, we need a landscape map of what each song looks and sounds like — in our mind's eye and the audience's ears.

Many of you reading this actually run your programs in three or four- year segments. Even though you may not know it or feel it, you are the lucky ones. Every three to four years, you have complete turnover in your singers (and their parents). This allows you more repetition of the things that have worked for you in your program and, hopefully, less repetition of the things that did not work.

Maps:
Three Year Map
One Year Map
Rehearsal Map
5-Minute Rehearsal Map
Song Map

Musical Maps

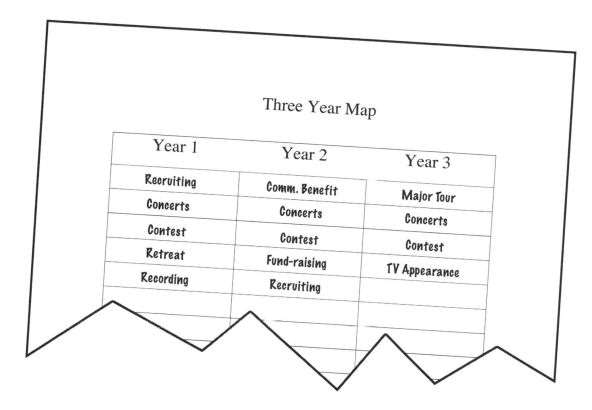

Three Year Map

Year 1	Year 2	Year 3
Recruiting	Comm. Benefit	Major Tour
Concerts	Concerts	Concerts
Contest	Contest	Contest
Retreat	Fund-raising	TV Appearance
Recording	Recruiting	

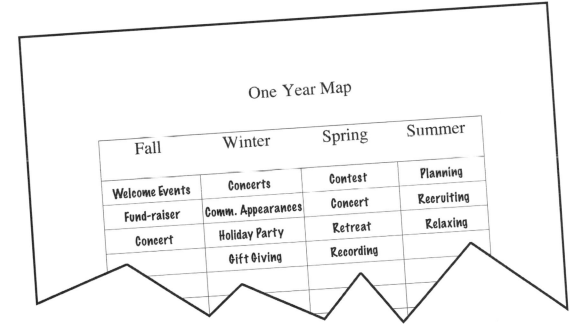

One Year Map

Fall	Winter	Spring	Summer
Welcome Events	Concerts	Contest	Planning
Fund-raiser	Comm. Appearances	Concert	Recruiting
Concert	Holiday Party	Retreat	Relaxing
	Gift Giving	Recording	

Rehearsal Map (Sample)

This is an 8-week sample plan of a very simple concert. Read it for the types of things that need to be included as the weeks progress. All points are usable in any situation and can be changed to a longer rehearsal period which hopefully most of you have!

April 1: Introduce concert – concept and repertoire.
Describe event, special features, etc.
Run through ALL of the music.
Pass out program order.
Focus on *America the Beautiful*.

April 8: Rehearse the concert music in order this week.
Memory Pop Quiz on *America the Beautiful*.
Focus on *God Bless America* and *The Star-Spangled Banner*.
Pass out "Cheat Sheets" (text only) for all repertoire.

April 15: Pass out promotion materials: posters, flyers, business cards, etc.
Memory: *America the Beautiful, The Star-Spangled Banner*.
Tell a little about and focus work on *O Canada*.
Focus on *The Testament of Freedom,* movements 1 and 4.

April 22: Give first report on PR efforts and ticket sales.
Memory pop quiz: *The Testament of Freedom* (similar to each other).
Solo auditions after rehearsal.

April 29: Sing concert in order.
Memory: *God Bless America*.
Have soloist finalists sing in rehearsal.

May 4: Sing entire concert from memory with "Cheat Sheets."
Go back over things that did not go as well as planned.

May 11: Add *Dona Nobis Pacem* – round with audience.
Work parts of program that still need attention.

May 18: Perform entire concert on risers - in order, no "Cheat Sheets."
Do all segues, solos, etc. with no stops and starts.
Add all instruments.

May 25: Dress Rehearsal
Remind the singers of why you are doing this concert.
Help them visualize the impact it is going to have on the audience and on them!

June 2: **CONCERT!**

Song Map
Sample, using Joseph Martin's "The Awakening."

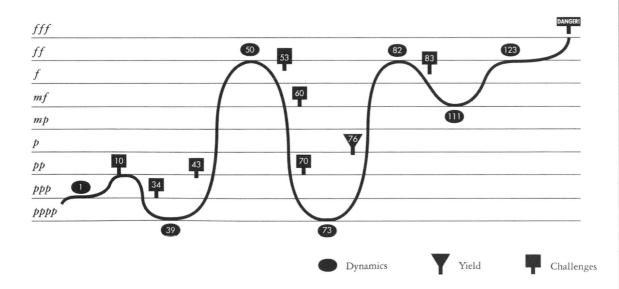

| | Dynamics | Yield | Challenges |

1. Set the dynamic range of the chorus so they know exactly where a quadruple "p" is in their voices and where the fortissimo is.

2. Vowel challenge: The i vowel in "Dream" is everywhere!

3. Keep the line going when the phrases are divided as in Measures 34–39.

4. Tuning challenge at Measure 43. Tune these chords.

5. Deal with the "bad" vowel at Measure 53.

6. Textual challenge: Diction in measure 60.

   - Whispering in measure 70
   - Yield! Each entering part must project. Those already singing must be quiet!
   - Legato and dynamic challenge: The last few pages are a challenge in several ways.

Chapter 3: Looking Around

Every situation is unique, or as we like to say with tongue firmly planted in cheek, "more unique." Of course, we all think our situation is more unique than the next, even though no such description exists. The physical requirements of each situation differ. However, just as in any profession, there is a minimum number of tools required to do the job. This is sometimes difficult to communicate to those who are actually responsible for providing most of those tools.

No one would call a plumber to their home and expect them to arrive with no tools, borrowing whatever you might have stashed beneath the kitchen sink to do the job. You would fire them on the spot. In addition to the heavy toll belts, they have trucks standing by with every possible tool of the trade.

We, as choral musicians, are somehow expected to have all of the tools we might need either in our head or attached to our bodies. We arrive to "fix the problem" and we are offered a few tools stashed somewhere in a storage cabinet or closet. Many may be marked "Only in case of emergency," or "No one has ever actually used this, but we'll keep it just in case."

The tools that are provided are rarely new — much less "state of the art" — and we don't "travel" with all of the things we need to be successful at our jobs. Many of them do go with us — our charm, our wit, our talent, our musicality, our charisma. But we definitely need help with the tools of the trade and we need those hiring us to understand that.

There are some jobs we can do just by showing up with a notebook of music and a pitch pipe. But those are few and far between. Referencing minimum standards set by others is helpful when discussing our needs with our bosses.

Many organizations have helped us with some of these standards. Some information from sources such as MENC can be helpful in making a list of "must have's." While serving as the Chairman of the Choral Advisory Committee for the Dallas Independent School District, our task was to get administrators to understand and accept our equipment needs. It is an ongoing dialogue!

Few of us walk into a situation where everything we could ever want is provided. And we certainly are not able to "travel" with all of the things we need. Some simply have to already be there.

Facilities — My Work Environment

This list came from the "Standards for Implementation for Music at the Secondary Level" set by the Texas Music Administrators Conference. Each state has the same information available. Here are some basics that should be standard anywhere.

- Music area should be sound isolated from other areas of the school.
- The main rehearsal area should be large enough to accommodate the largest group that ultimately will use the room.
- Minimum height of the rehearsal room should be 16 feet.
- A reliable and preferably independent system of climate control is essential including circulation of air.
- Adequate lighting is needed in all rehearsal and work areas.
- Each choral rehearsal hall should have seated risers.
- Each choral rehearsal hall should have choral chairs for the students, not desks.
- A separate room, with locks, should be provided for uniform storage, library, and sound equipment.
- Each rehearsal room should include a lockable office for the music director and needs a telephone line for after-school hours, as well as during the school day.
- Each choral rehearsal facility should include a minimum of one sound-insulated practice room.
- The choral rehearsal hall is not to be used for other classes.

Equipment — Nuts and Bolts

Everyone in our business should have a list of tools required to do their jobs. They are things that you should check on before accepting a job. Even if all are not provided, at least those in places of authority will be advised of what you need, whether they provide them or not!

These are from the MENC "Opportunity to Learn: Standards for Music Instruction." Take these and make a list for yourself.

High-quality sound system (recording and playback)
CD-ROM compatible computers
MIDI equipment
Music library file cabinets
Shelving
High-quality acoustic piano (tuned 3 times a year)
Risers
Choral chairs
Conductor's stand, podium, music stand
Choral shell (where needed)

Other items on our "wish" list:

White board
Choral robes/wardrobe
Costumes
Folders
Music
Recordings
Photography
Videography
Fees for clinicians
Choreographer
Travel opportunities
Instrumentalists
A raise

Adding Singers

You've done all of the extremely important work of preparation. You have prepared yourself and your work environment. You have planned for every possible eventuality. You are excited and enthusiastic about what is to come.

It's almost time to add the singers. There is a great deal of information available to assist in getting singers to join you. However, there is nothing so powerful in recruitment as **"lunchroom buzz."** When your singers leave rehearsal and meet their friends, do they drag into the lunchroom or restaurant complaining "I am so tired and bored. I just came from the worst part of my week – choir. Would you like to join?" On the other hand, do they leave your rehearsals humming, singing, skipping, having been inspired and energized by being under your tutelage? If so, their friends won't need any encouragement to join.

You've done your other recruiting activities. You've posted flyers. You've spread the word far and wide about choir. Best of all, the "lunchroom buzz" has been really good. You've been to the feeder schools or organizations to meet potential singers. The first day of choir is always an exciting time, regardless of what kind of choir you conduct or how long you have been doing it. Singers arrive with new "supplies," sharpened pencils and minds, and are eager to sing.

Have you done everything you can to make choir the special thing it truly is? According to Abraham Maslow's hierarchy of human needs, singing in choir covers at least seven of the eight basic needs! You can find this list in "The Perfect Rehearsal." The first need is biological: food, air, and water. The second is safety. Have you created a safe place for your singers? Singing in public is a frightening thing – they take a risk every time they open their mouths to sing for you. Do they love singing for you?

What are they saying about choir and about you as the conductor? If it is good, you won't have any recruitment issues. Hopefully, you are in a situation where you are able to audition singers for your choir. Following is a sample audition form you might use and a list of rehearsal expectations to pass out to those you accept. Both are excellent tools.

Audition Form

Date _____

Name _____

Birth Date _____

Address _____

_____

E-mail (please print) _____

Phone #'s   (H) _____   (W) _____
                 (C) _____

Voice part you have sung before (circle) :
S1 S2 A1 A2 T1 T2 Baritone Bass

How many years experience do you have in the following area?
Private Voice _____   Choir _____   Piano _____

Theatre Experience:

Instruments you play or have played:

Education:

Choral groups in which you have sung:

What singers do you enjoy listening to?

encoura

REHEARSAL EXPECTATIONS

1. Singers are expected to treat the conductor/teacher and each other with utmost respect. Singing is a very personal and often vulnerable activity.

2. Each singer should be in their chair or on the risers prepared to begin rehearsal on time. Being late causes you to miss a portion of warm-ups, limiting your ability to get the most out of rehearsal. Rehearsal isn't over when the singer thinks it is, but rather when the conductor says it's over.

3. Turn off "noisemakers" (watches, cell phones, etc.) before rehearsal begins.

4. Keep talking to a minimum.

5. Have your folder with music and a pencil in hand during every rehearsal. A pencil in a book bag across the room, or a folder with music at home is insufficient. Expect periodic "pencil, sight-reading, and memory checks."

6. The singer remains personally responsible for the condition of the choir folder and music once it is distributed.

7. Singers are expected to remain actively engaged in the rehearsal at all times. There is always room for improvement in individual performance. Hard work is expected. It is not optional. Keep talking to a minimum (worth repeating).

8. Follow directions....the first time they are given. Positive and cooperative attitudes result in a fun and productive atmosphere. Don't ask why, just do it!

9. Upon receiving music, singers should number all measures, using a pencil only, and make marks in their music as instructed by the conductor.

10. Singers are responsible for the care of the choir room. When rehearsal is completed, put all supplies away, throw away trash, and take all personal items with you as you leave.

11. STAY INFORMED by updating your personal calendar! Listen; read all communications for updates; check the calendar; ask, if you are unsure of something. The more involved you are, the more fun choir can become.

Where Should They Sit?

There are as many answers to this as there are singers – and certainly as many as there are choral conductors. And everyone has the "magic" seating chart that will turn your somewhat mediocre choir into Grammy Award-winners, if you will just abide by their recommendations.

Some years ago, there was a detailed study reported in the *Choral Journal* about every possible seating arrangement on the planet. The conclusion was pretty much that there are many options that will work. The most important finding was that each singer needs enough space to "hear" the sound they are making, while integrating that sound into that of those around them. Due to space limitations, this is not always possible when the chorus is quite large, but most of the time we have the luxury of space. Rather than gather our singers in a tight clump, like cows under a tree on a hot day, we need to spread them out in whatever space we have available. This has been made clear by the great choirs of our day. We don't always trust that it will work for our amateur (in the best sense of the word) singers. But it will.

Assigned seating works in smaller groups and in what one might call nonvolunteer groups. My experience has been that people who are volunteering their time and spending a great deal of their time in rehearsals are fairly certain who they want to sit by and who they don't. Even though assigned seating can improve the sound, there is some compromise on our part as conductors.

Our main energy is spent on education, creativity, and organization. As long as we can educate our singers as to the importance of seating, they will cooperate (up to a point). We can also be organized and creative in moving the singers around in order to allow them the opportunity to hear other sounds throughout the choir. This serves to help enhance the end result and their musicianship as well.

Move them around. Don't get stuck! There is more than one answer! One size does not fit all.

Sample Seating Charts

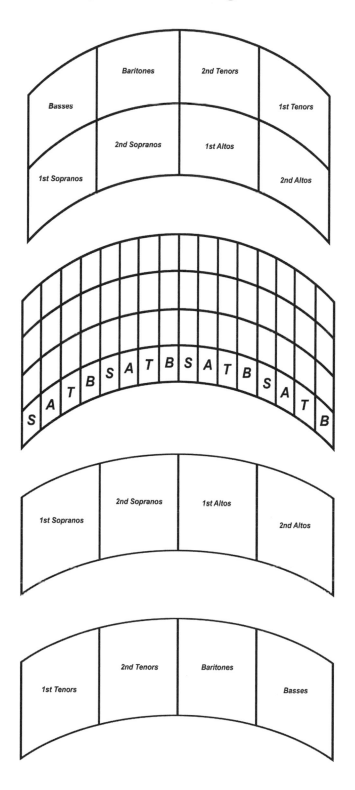

Chapter 4: Looking Inside...The Music

What sets us apart?

My musical career began in junior high school playing string bass in the orchestra, not singing in the school choir. Actually, I was quite chubby as a teenager and I think I chose the string bass because it was the only instrument that I could hide behind. Nonetheless, it provided a fantastic foundation upon which the rest of my years would be built.

It wasn't long, however, before my true self longed to get out from behind that bass and the music stand and SING! And I never looked back. Adding communication through text was something that could never again be separated from my music making.

Communicating the text is the most important thing we do as choral musicians. Period. If we are not focused on communicating with our audience, we may as well be bowling!

Each time I conduct a chorus with orchestral accompaniment, I think I see myself in every player – hiding behind the music stand, looking up only when absolutely necessary. It may be one of the deep-seated reasons that I will not allow my choruses to use music. No hiding! All of our singers have plenty of the brain cells required for memorization.

My colleague, Pam Elrod, has provided a fantastic guide to teaching the text to our choirs, which she in turn obtained from her studies with Dr. Robert Bode at Whitman College. It is exceptional and I am most grateful to share it with you here. In addition, she has provided detailed descriptions of other ways to study each song we are to conduct.

Teaching the Text

Just as the chorus has agreed on the manner of production of the musical elements in a piece of music, it must also be on the same page regarding all aspects of the text. Here are some steps to assist with that:

1. Give some information about the genesis of the text and biographical information about the author.
2. Have the text read out loud by one person or the entire group.
3. Ask the singers what the text means to them.
5. Provide a translation if in a foreign language.
6. Assign one beat to each syllable and chant in unison.
7. Work on the prosody — natural speech pattern.
8. Point out accented vs. unaccented syllables.
9. Sing the song on one vowel.
10. Sing the song on vowels only — no consonants, and insist on absolute purity of vowels.
11. Sing the song with words.
12. Ask half of the choir to sing text and the rest to count-sing (counters should be the predominating texture). Switch periodically.
13. Ask half of the choir to sing on a nonsense syllable such as "loo" or "nah" and the rest sing text.

Other tips:
- Every syllable in every language has a beginning, a middle, and an end, each of which must be pronounced clearly and correctly.
- Parts of syllables can be "rhythmicized"; consequently, text is joined with rhythm before it is joined with proper pitches.
- Initiating vowels must occur on their respective beats or sub-beats.
- Consonants that precede these vowels must occur in advance.
- No American "r" should ever be heard in a foreign language.
- Teach the text in small sections rather than the entire piece.
- Text can be added to the texture of the music in several ways:
  1. Homophonic texture — text is sung with proper rhythms on a unison pitch.
  2. Contrapuntal texture — text is sung with proper rhythms on a whole-tone cluster.

Be sure to check out the additional B.o.B.s on the CD:

- How to Study a Song
- Bar Analysis
- Pedagogical Analysis

Chapter 5: It's Time to Rehearse

You have 20 people in a room who don't know each other. That presents a particular set of issues. Or perhaps you have 200 people in a room that know each other. That presents a completely different set of issues. If you are conducting middle school students, you have hormonal issues entering into play. If you are conducting an aging church choir, you have hormonal issues that enter into play. In between those two are a myriad of dysfunctional possibilities.

How are we going to maintain order and keep peace and quiet while we ply our art? Good question. Many books have been written on this topic. One of my colleagues offered a great suggestion. She asked her singers to sign contracts at the beginning of the rehearsal period. Of course, if it is a school situation, there are punitive measures that can be taken (there's nothing more motivating to learning your music than a heavy paddle — just kidding). But there are some things in place in an educational setting that aren't available in community and church choirs — like a grade or guilt.

Putting the responsibility back on the singer is the perfect thing to do. No one wants to volunteer their time with a parole officer or bouncer standing in the back of the room. Try having your singers sign a **Self-Management Contract** such as the one you will find on the CD-ROM.

Planning Rehearsals

Ask your singers to put their music in concert order as best you know it. It will save time in rehearsal. In addition, if you rehearse it in order, you begin to get a feel for the flow of the concert. I always recommend that everyone begin with a plan divided into 5-minute increments. Not only does it keep the singers engaged in what they are doing, they will love rehearsals and the time will fly.

This will work in every situation — for a 30-minute rehearsal or a weekend retreat with 16 hours of rehearsal! If you need more time on a specific piece, simply mark out three 5-minute increments to really dig into it. But no more than three. If you really feel you need to work longer on one piece, then do it in two completely separate 15-minute increments, with something else in between to keep your singers interested.

In addition, the 5-minute plan is a great fix to discipline in rehearsal — they just don't have time to do anything but focus on you! You know that dead space when you are trying to think of what to do next is most often when you lose them. The 5-minute plan helps you stay ahead of them.

We should always be striving to use new technology to aid us in rehearsals. E-mail information to your singers in advance to avoid taking up useful rehearsal time. Use podcasts to communicate with them (and your audience). Put music out there as mp3s or on YouTube. Put your choreography in Wave files for them to practice at home.

Make sure you also put TLC into your rehearsals, just as you do in your performances. Of course, that means Tender Loving Care, but more importantly, a Tear, a Laugh and a Chill bump. We are there to be a family. We are there to have a good time and laugh. We are there to create musical magic through the choral art — even in rehearsal — or especially in rehearsal. If it doesn't happen in rehearsal, chances are it won't happen in performance.

See B.o.B. for the 5-Minute Rehearsal Plan.

How to Warm Up

Readers of my first book, "The Perfect Blend," already know I am completely focused on vocal technique and warming up a chorus (shameless plug). So, a frequently asked question is, "How long should you spend warming up your chorus?" My answer: "However long your rehearsal is!" The first two syllables of "Rehearsal" are "Re-Hear" for good reason!

Every time your chorus meets, you must do at least one exercise from each of the following groups and in the following order. Of course, you are more than welcome to do more than one from each, if you have time. But you must do one from each group every time, not skipping a single one or taking them out of order.

Here are the five "food groups" of warming up:

Appetizer – Posture
Soup – Breathing
Salad – Phonation
Entrée – Resonance
Dessert – Blend!

Preparing your chorus to sing is one of the most important things a choral director can do. The difficulty lies in the fact that you have 20 or 200 people in front of you, each in a different state of readiness to sing, and each at a different level of experience. Your task is to find a median from which all of them can benefit. This is an enormous challenge.

START WITH BIG MUSCLE GROUPS AND WORK DOWN!

Singing should be an athletic endeavor. After all, when done properly, it involves the entire body. There is no other athletic event where a person would arrive and simply begin. Every other type of activity begins with stretching. If you hire a trainer, they will always start with big muscle groups. But even before that, you are going to have to stretch! That nice, thin trainer will sit in the corner and ask you to do lunges across the room until your legs are shaky and you think you can't walk. <u>That</u> is starting with the big muscle groups.

And what do we, as leaders of vocal athletes, do? Our singers gather in a room and start with the smallest muscle we can think of — the vocal folds! This trend simply must be reversed. Warm-ups begin with the individual's needs (big muscle groups, massage, getting the body awake, etc.) and only then move toward the posture, breath, and finally, the vocal folds.

When I conduct workshops, the singers are told that they should never do a warm-up for which they do not know the purpose. Permission is given to kindly raise their hands and ask the conductor what a particular exercise is supposed to teach them. This sometimes causes great consternation for the conductors whose only answer is "because my high school choir teacher used it." It also causes those to sweat who either never thought of the "why" or who are just using the exercises as a "filler" or to kill time. "Killing time" is not an answer I would suggest you use, regardless of how true.

your books, papers, and notes from college, collecting all of the
ou can. Categorize them according to the five groups as I have done
book. Most importantly, figure out what each one of them achieves
ding of vocal or choral technique, so you can answer that inquisitive
singer who wants to know why they are being asked to do this exercise.
ber:

OU MAY BE THE ONLY VOICE TEACHER MANY OR OST OF YOUR CHORUS MEMBERS HAVE EVER HAD!

Musical Mishaps

Saving Your Rehearsal From Being "DOA"

Nothing can kill a rehearsal more quickly or thoroughly than chasing notes. As you know, it is often a person who is not missing the note at all, but wants to make sure everyone knows that they know that someone is missing a note. Most often it's a 2nd tenor.

There are many ways to avoid killing rehearsal, such as having the other sections humming while the section in question (most often the 2nd tenors) are working on their notes.

However, the most effective tool I have ever seen or used is for every choir member to have access to the **"Musical Mishap"** form. They are encouraged to fill this out when someone in their section is consistently missing a note and turn it in to the appropriate people. This way, the conductor can gather them together and go over the specific problem areas at the next rehearsal – if he/she deems it necessary.

This form gives each singer an investment into the improvement of the chorus and a tool with which to communicate their issues without interrupting rehearsal.

Production Planning

No doubt you have probably already found that there is almost no such thing as too much planning. To repeat, each rehearsal needs to be planned in 5-minute increments to keep it flowing, to keep you on track, and to keep your singers engaged.

All too often, I have been at rehearsals late in the rehearsal period where everyone was called, or expected to be there at the very beginning. Then the conductor decides how to proceed from there, keeping everyone for the entire time whether they are involved or not. This may work for choruses made up of children or students, but certainly not adults — it is a waste of their time.

Those of us who have been involved in professional opera, theater, or symphonic worlds know that when companies are in rehearsal, they plan much better than we sometimes do in the choral world. Most often, rehearsals are called starting with the pieces that involve the largest number of people and then participants are released as they are no longer needed.

There is no point in making everyone arrive at the beginning of rehearsal and having them sit through solos, small groups, transitions, etc. And a choral group should not have to sit through a tech rehearsal meant only for lighting and sound people. Of course, in most instances other than the choral world, there is a "dark" night between final dress and opening night. Choruses often don't plan far enough ahead to have the luxury of nights off between final rehearsals and the performance. Dress rehearsal should absolutely be in order and with no starts and stops. It should be as close to the performance as possible.

Sit down with your "helpers," whether they be paid staff or volunteers, before you get to the final rehearsals. Work with them on a minute by minute rundown of the tech rehearsal, dress rehearsal, and the actual concert — including all transitions, applause, etc. Use actual timings of songs. Discuss how much talking there will be – listen to them!

Using such a minute by minute script will help everyone involved in the production of your concert. Don't give it to the singers. They don't need to know your plan — just that you have one! It will also help you avoid being surprised that the concert is too long!

Tech Script
(sample)

6:30	Walk-through on stage – all participants
	"Cue to Cue" – meaning start and finish each song – chorus exits
7:30	Open doors to house
	Backstage "share" time with singers
7:45:	Organ music begins preconcert
7:55:	House lights to half
	Chamber chorus enters stage – right and left
	Full chorus down the aisles/Trumpet quartet enters choral terrace
7:59	Percussion, accompanists, conductor enter
8:00	Downbeat - *Personent Hodie*
	Applause – brass remains in place
	Lights out on choral terrace (quartet)
8:07	*Dona Nobis Pacem* (mood lighting – special on oboe)
	Oboe solo
8:11	**Segue** – *Ding Dong* – horn quartet
	Chorus moves to the stage
8:13	*Joy to the World*
	saxophone; Lonnie Parks solo; percussion
	Applause
	Welcome to audience – thank you – intro to next piece
8:18	*O Holy Night*
	Applause
8:22	*Making Spirits Bright*
	Percussion, piano, saxophone solo
	Santa enters during this number
	Applause
8:27	*Greensleeves* – saxophone solo
	Applause
8:31	*Lux Arumque*
	Segue (ENCORE – exit on intro)
8:35	*Little Drummer Boy*
	Percussion, piano and organ.
	Applause – ENCORE enters
8:39	*Annoying Drummer Boy*
	Piano
	Applause
8:43	Intermission speech/announcements
8:46	*Yuletide Rhythm*
	Applause
8:50	Intermission
9:05	Organ prelude to 2nd half

9:10 – 2nd half begins
10:05 – 2nd half ends

Final Notes to Self

1. Do I have the right music folder?
2. Is it in order?
3. Do I have all of the notes, announcements, segues, etc. written in?
4. Have I planned carefully when the audience will applaud and when there will be a segue?
5. Have I planned all stage moves/adjustments so there is NO dead space for the audience?
6. Have I planned when I will bow and when the chorus will bow – and any special groups, soloists, guests?
7. Have I expressed my gratitude to the singers and offered congratulations for their hard work?
8. Have I thanked everyone who has helped get us to this point, such as accompanists, instrumentalists, stage hands, etc.?
9. Prior to the concert, have I allowed the singers some time to express themselves about who they may have in the audience or what they may have experienced during the rehearsal period leading up to the concert?
10. Do I have a handkerchief handy in case there is something greater than "glowing" (that would be sweat)?
11. Do I have some breath mints handy for when I greet the adoring fans after the concert?
12. Have I looked at my back in a 2-way mirror to make sure there is not some unsightly wardrobe malfunction that the audience will have to look at all night?

Thirty Minutes To Curtain

The day has come for the performance. Your singers arrive, ready to go. You spend time with them going over final notes, warming them up, talking through the concert, and perhaps even one last "cue to cue" rundown of the program. It is too late to fix anything major. So, now is a good time to remind them of a few details. At this point, they are likely to remember a few well-placed instructions. More importantly, however, it is time to focus on the big picture of what you are about to do.

Whatever your preperformance schedule is, reserve 30 minutes to meet with them backstage or in a rehearsal room. The excitement is palpable. The singers have a million things on their minds including how they look, who is in the audience, and where they are going to eat after the concert.

Help them imagine what the emotional roller coaster will be. Help them empathize with what the audience is going to hear and experience. Assign colors or adjectives to each song to give them an idea of the big picture so everyone is on the same page.

Save your best shot for the pep talk; our "huddle" before taking the field. This is where you transform from coach to cheerleader! Once again, if you are uncomfortable doing the "touchy-feely," then you must get someone else to do it. Do not simply leave it out because it is not in your comfort zone.

Allow the singers to speak. Direct the comments. Ask them what this concert means to them. Ask if there are specific songs that mean something personal. Ask if they have special guests in the audience they would like to speak about. These brief moments unify the group and give them an even deeper sense of investment.

Touching each other is a good thing. Ask them to touch someone on the shoulder – or hold hands. Feeling the unity and energy, bringing weeks and weeks of hard work to a culmination, is an important exercise.

Invite them to step right up to the emotional line you have practiced. Take a moment of silence and then guide their thoughts to the miracle of communicating with the audience through the music. Then, say "Break a leg" and cross your fingers!

Chapter 6: Communication

We've all heard it over and over. There is nothing that will solve problems as well as effective and consistent communication. Most often, that means communication in advance, not after the fact. In many aspects of our lives and professions, less is more. This is not one of those. In this instance, there can hardly be too much communication.

There is, of course, no guarantee that the intended recipients will actually interpret your communication. That is not the point. There is also a danger that if you send too much information, or too often, they will just tune you out or ignore you. The more simple your communication is, the better.

Everything you need to communicate to your singers can be posted on a Web site for them to read at their leisure. Communication is why we are in the arts to begin with. Communication is why we chose choral music as opposed to instrumental music. Communication with our audience when we perform is hopefully utmost in our minds.

Communication can be divided into several areas:

1. From the singers to you – Productivity Tool
2. From you to the singers – Tim's Notes
3. From you to your employers – Artistic Director's Report
4. From your chorus to the world – Press Release

There are many times when ample communication has saved my hide. When a singer says, "You didn't tell us what to wear to the mall to sing," or "No one told me there was a deposit due for going on the trip," or "I didn't know we were singing at the mall and I certainly didn't know what time" How wonderful it is to be able to simply say, "Well, precious, that information was e-mailed out eight weeks ago and has been posted on the chorus web site since then. Bless your heart." And you can say it with a loving smile.

Productivity Tool

In order to make productive and constructive suggestions, I would like to make the following observation regarding:

_____ Officers   ✔ Board of Directors

✔ Artistic Staff   _____ Administrative Staff

_____ Associates   _____ Others (Please Specify)

My view of the problem:

rehearsals are boring!

A solution I would like to offer:

artistic staff work on rehearsal plan in advance rather than just winging it.

Read "The Perfect Rehearsal"

Others who support my suggestion (NOT REQUIRED):

John, Bob, Ted, Alice, and Betty

Signed: _T̃m̃ S̃ẽl̃ỹ_

If you would like to write something on your own instead of using this form, feel free to do so. Please remember to include your suggested solution to the problem.

Conductor's Notes

Communication is whatever tool you use to keep your singers informed of all of the details it takes to run a choral program. It is the method for disseminating all information without having to tell them from the podium.

In the olden days, we actually copied these notes to distribute at rehearsal and then mailed hard copies to every singer who was absent. Gone are those days in this almost "paperless" society. They are now e-mailed and our singers have multiple e-mail addresses, FaceBook, MySpace, beepers, iPhones, etc.

As I said earlier, more is better. You surely have had many times when singers have said, "You didn't tell us we were supposed to be at the concert hall an hour early." Or more often, "You didn't tell us we were supposed to wear our formal attire." Or, "You didn't tell us to bring our music to rehearsal." And on and on it goes.

Sending out e-notes and posting them on the chorus web site will cover all of those questions. Now, just as many of them don't listen in rehearsal and many don't read either. But when they show up late for the concert, in the wrong outfit, and with no music, it is certainly not because the information wasn't out there. In fact, it is still out there so they can go home and realize there is no one to blame but themselves.

In your notes, always start with the most important and most current information, just as you do when writing a press release. Keep it as simple as possible. Tell them where to be, when to be there, what to wear, and what they need to bring.

As the notes continue, you can then add other information that you would like to share with them. This is the perfect place to keep them informed of the exciting things that are coming up in the future and the nice things that people are saying about the chorus or organization.

Tim's Notes

"Behold the turtle. He makes progress only when he sticks his neck out."

Date: Jan. 10, 2008

This Week:
Sectional rehearsal on Sunday afternoon, 4:00 – 6:00 p.m., Grace United Methodist Church. Work on foreign language and choralography!

Memory:
Pop quiz on the two German pieces on Sunday.

Committee Meetings:
Fund Development on Thursday evening. See Web site for details.

Concert tickets are on sale now! The concert is only 5 weeks away. Please pick up your flyers, posters, and post cards. Next week, we will have business cards to advertise the concert.

Outreach:
A week from Saturday, we will be singing a mini-concert for the Women's Shelter to help them raise money. Please sign up tonight if you are able to sing.

Finances:
Your deposit is due for the trip to Waxahachie! Get that money in.

Wardrobe:
Get your formal attire ready for the concert. Make sure you have your choir t-shirt washed to wear for singing at the mall.

Next Week:
We'll be singing without "Cheat Sheets" on risers.

Kudos! We received many wonderful comments from the last concert. I will attach those to the next e-mail.

Artistic Director's Report

Everyone has someone to whom they report. It may be a principal, supervisor or board of directors. Sometimes we think that simply putting on excellent concerts or doing well at contests should be enough for them. Well, it isn't. This book lists several tools for evaluating your job performance on several levels. However, one of the best ways to do that is through a report you generate yourself. Remember: No one is going to toot your horn for you! You have to toot it yourself!

This doesn't have to be in an obnoxious or boastful manner, but in a simple, informative way. How many times have I heard the comment about choral directors, "I wonder what they do during the week?" While this sends us completely off the charts in frustration, we have to take some of the blame. Of course, some of that can be found in the list of "roles" we supply to our singers (other than conductor) listed earlier in the book.

However, a very useful exercise is for you and your superiors to keep track of the things you do outside the rehearsal hall and away from the concert stage. Once again, it is a form you will keep on your computer. Each month (or at whatever time period required), you simply complete and distribute it to the appropriate persons. Keeping up with it won't take much time to complete if the weekly notes you send to the singers and/or parents are used.

The one area you do not include in the weekly notes to the singers are your activities within the community and the networking you do in order to be more successful at your job. What meetings did you attend? What groups do you belong to? What offices do you hold in professional organizations? What networking opportunities did you initiate or participate in? What other kinds of activities did you do that enhanced your capabilities? Did you take a course? Did you attend a workshop?

Bottom line, keep tabs on yourself. Don't be bashful. You'd be surprised who thinks you are playing golf or eating bonbons!

Artistic Director's Board Report – April, 2007

The preparation for the next concert is going well. We can use your help in selling tickets and advertising for the program.

Performances/Outreach:

The full chorus is singing for the Women's Shelter this month.

The small ensemble was able to perform for 3 different events: 2 benefits and one for an honorarium.

Community Relations:

Held luncheon for area conductors to share ideas.

Met with financial officers from two corporation

discuss possible fund   the choru

Family meeting to go o

Press Release

World Choir

P.O. Box 55555 Dallas, Texas 75555 ... 214-555-1234 ... 214-555-123(tax)
www.worldchoir.com

News

World Choir Takes Tour To The Moon
First Ever Concerts In Gravity-free Environment

Dallas, Texas-November 12, 2007 – The World Choir, based in Dallas, Texas, is the first to have landed on the moon and promptly given a concert. The amazing effect of so many singers singing in gravity suits had a profound effect on the individuals.

Problem-Solving — General

Wouldn't it be great if we could just float through our careers and lives, never encountering problems? Well, that doesn't happen for anyone, and certainly doesn't happen for those of us in positions of leadership who are in the creative arts. Art is subjective by its very nature.

There is little in our profession that can be guaranteed, but conflict is 100 percent so. There are many reasons for this. One is that we are involved in something about which people are very passionate. That is a double-edged sword. We want to provide a flame that attracts people to us as moths to a flame, but we have also seen what happens to those who get too close to the flame. They are lucky if only singed.

Our art is also very personal. Singing is one of the most vulnerable of all the arts. In using our voices to communicate with others, the connection can become very intimate. One of the most perfect descriptions I have ever heard about singers is that we possess a "wide emotional palette." Well, that is the understatement. Additionally, we can be seen as swinging on that completely bipolar yard swing between complete confidence and complete fragility.

We are not the easiest people to live with, either. How often have we put spouses or family members in that no-win situation of asking "How did I do?" rather than waiting for a thoughtful response when we were more ready to receive their answer? How often did we really hope they would lie to us rather than speak the truth? The famous movie quote comes to mind, "You can't handle the truth." We certainly can't handle it immediately following a performance.

There are two other great tools that can assist us with conflict:

1) Those dealing with **personal conflict** with singers, colleagues,
    associates, etc.
2) Those concerning potential **organizational conflict** – with our superiors
    or colleagues.

Problem Solving — Personal

The following list is one that can be used in conflicts with people other than your boss or bosses. These kinds of guides can be found in many places with various outcomes. Take this one, change it as you wish, and put it up on your wall.

1. Breathe deeply.
2. Count to a number much larger than 10.
3. Sleep on it.
4. Do not accept any "hearsay" as fact.
5. Accept other's feelings as their reality.
6. Celebrate diversity of experiences and ideas.
7. Develop a constructive outcome.
8. When you are calm, go first to the source.
9. If not comfortable talking to the person, then try the person's supervisor or my supervisor.
10. Get confirmation of the facts if necessary.
11. Determine how to resolve the problem.
12. Determine how to avoid the problem in the future.
13. If you have not completed steps 1 – 11, keep your concerns and opinions to yourself!

Problem Solving — Organizational

The Importance of Communication. Solving problems when they first develop is recommended. Open and effective communication is the answer to most problems, resolving them before they significantly impact anyone involved. An employee should feel free to discuss his or her problems with his/her immediate supervisor and thereby give the supervisor an opportunity to resolve them without resorting to the procedures set forth below.

1st Step: Verbal Discussion with Supervisor. An employee who believes he or she has been unfairly treated, or wishes to correct any misunderstanding, should first discuss such matters with his or her immediate supervisor. Normally the employee's supervisor will be able to resolve the matter equitably and to the employee's satisfaction.

2nd Step: Written Appeal to Personnel or Human Services. If the problem has not been resolved, the employee may seek a solution from Personnel or Human Services. The employee must submit a written statement to the above within three working days of discussing the problem with his or her supervisor. The designated person will discuss the problem with the employee and the supervisor. An answer will be given within ten working days.

3rd Step: Written Appeal to Board of Directors. If the problem has not been resolved with the first and second steps discussed above, such employee may request a solution from the Board of Directors. Such employee must submit a written statement within three working days of receiving the response from Personnel or Human Services. The Board of Directors will have ten days to review the problem and make a decision in writing. The Board Chair or his or her designee will give such employee an answer in writing. This decision will be final.

Money Management

One of the things we perhaps weren't told in college was that we would need to be accountants once we were out of school and started work. Not only accountants, but good money managers and planners.

Most of us are responsible for the budget for our music programs. This takes some real juggling in today's world of budget cuts in arts education and the competitive market place for our concerts.

In addition to our personal finances, we are required to keep tabs on thousands of dollars in things such as wardrobe, fund-raising, music purchase, fees, etc. The knowledge of Excel is invaluable, even though it is not something that falls into the curriculum of a music major.

There are many aspects of our lives in which we need to be good money managers. Of course, one of those is in our personal lives. Because our days are filled with activities, many of which we hope are paid, we have the additional task of figuring out the tax implications on having a full-time job as well as the many jobs that may give us additional income. This is when you need the advice of a good CPA to help protect yourself. The rules change every year, so it is definitely worth having someone help us who is accustomed to working with choral directors. Amazing things can be deducted, such as dry cleaning, music purchase, attending concerts, travel, part of your home as an office/studio, etc. It will pay to have professional help and advice.

Have several budget forms handy so that you can fill one out for each year and each event. You can add or subtract from them depending on the particular needs. Take them and make them your own.

The first is an actual budget for a series of holiday concerts. You will see we exceeded budget in places and came under in others to make the budget balance.

Concert Budget (Sample)

Expenses

Item	Budget	Actual
Concert Venue	$25,000	$30,500
Rehearsal Venue	$1,500	$1,500
Costumes/Wardrobe	$2,000	$1,300
Instrument Rental	$2,500	$3,100
(Piano, Organ, etc.)		
Choreographer	$2,000	$2,000
Musicians/Performers	$10,500	$7,350
(Chamber Orchestra, etc.)		
Recording	$2,000	$2,000
Video - $1,500		
Audio - $500		
Compositions/Arrangements	$5,000	$4,200
Music Purchase	$6,000	$4,900
ASCAP/BMI	$2,700	$2,700
Lighting/Sound	$1,000	$3,000
Staging/Sets/Props	$6,500	$5,300
(Risers, decorations, shell)		
Security for rehearsals	$1,500	$1,500
Copying	$1,000	$500
(Notes, etc.)		
Contract Variable	$1,500	$1500
(Riser crew, signer, etc.)		
Program Printing		
Advertising		
Miscellaneous Expense	$1,000	$0
(Flowers, gifts for the conductor)		
CONCERT TOTAL	**$71,700**	**$71,350**

Income:

Ticket sales	$75,000
Advertising sales	$15,000
Donations	$25,000
Underwriting	$10,000

Chapter 7: After the Concert

One thing we are sometimes least attentive to is what immediately follows a concert – at least as far as our singers are concerned. Of course, we tell them they did a great job and that they were awesome and never sounded better. But do we share comments from others? We are apt to forget that we are out front receiving compliments from a host of people while our singers may be backstage breaking down the risers, cleaning up, checking in music, etc., or they may be getting on the bus to return to school or have family responsibilities.

We, on the other hand, bask in the kudos, forgetting to pass them along to the singers. The e-mails, notes, and phone calls we receive following the performance need to be shared with the singers — well, at least the good ones. If someone calls, ask them to put their comments in writing and send them to you so you may share them with the singers. You never know how important that is to them. Many will save the comments for the rest of their lives.

You can certainly share with them the things that they can improve upon – but wait an appropriate amount of time before doing that. They will remember the first things you say – make sure they are positive.

One reminder: when you pass on kudos, make sure that they do not reflect poorly on other choirs, other singers, organizations or the chorus before you got there. This is not necessary to make the current group feel validated.

Post-Concert Journal

Conductors are not known as the most objective people on earth about our own work. In some ways, this is not completely our fault. We hear our choruses on the first day of each rehearsal period, season or school year. We then hear their progress each step of the way (under our remarkable tutelage). When the performance finally comes along, it is judged based on what we heard the first day of rehearsals. The audience wasn't there on that first day when we thought, "It's going to be a long year!"

The audience is hearing the chorus with fresh ears. All they have to base their assessment on is what they are hearing right now compared to what they remember from the last time the chorus performed, or the last performance they heard from a different chorus.

At these times we must find a way to be honest with ourselves. And this shouldn't just be after performances; it should also happen after rehearsals. Some questions could be asked after every rehearsal and at the very least, asked after a rehearsal period and certainly after the performance.

Post-Concert Journal Questions

1. What were my first impressions?
2. What were my impressions the next day?
3. What were my impressions the next week?
4. Do I feel the concert achieved its stated objectives?
5. Did this experience move my own journey forward? In what ways?
6. Did this experience affect the lives of the singers? In what ways?
7. Did this experience affect the lives of the audience? In what ways?
8. Am I listening to everyone and taking everything they are saying seriously?
9. Am I only listening to those people who are saying nice things about the concert and me?
10. Have I trusted the right people to tell me the truth?
11. Which of the "best ever" comments have validity and why?
12. How can I repeat these things?
13. Which of the criticisms have validity and what can I do to use them constructively?
14. Am I focused on the one critical review instead of the hundreds of positive ones?

How do others think I'm doing?

Once again, my colleague, Pam Elrod, provides us with a form for evaluation: **"Conducting Observation."** This is a tool she uses in observing conductors she is teaching, mentoring, or observing. It is a wonderful and comprehensive evaluation and covers every aspect of conducting.

We would be delusional to think we could actually make an objective assessment of our own conducting using this form. We just don't see ourselves for what we actually are and do. However, it is a necessary exercise and well worth the time and energy to have someone occasionally videotape us in a rehearsal. Sit down with the tape and use this form to evaluate yourself. I know I have some whopper bad habits. Some I intend to break, but others are accepted at this point as being part of who I am (denial runs deep and is not just a river in Egypt). At my age, they are simply "quirks" and written off as eccentric.

Find a colleague you trust and ask them to attend one of your rehearsals. Give them the checklist and ask them to fill it out. In return, you'll do the same for them. Just reading it is an important reminder of those things we were graded on when we were in school and is also a great tool to use should someone ask us to mentor them as they work on their own conducting. If you know a young student considering a career in conducting, it would help them become acquainted with the broad spectrum of the attributes of a fine conductor.

Regardless of how you use it – on yourself, on others or allowing others to use it on you, it is priceless.

CONDUCTING OBSERVATIONS

Conductor Observed_____

Date_____

Group_____

Rehearsal/Performance (circle one)

Works Performed (composer/title):

1)

2)

3)

4)

Rating Explanation
1. Excellent   2. Adequate   3. Needs Work

I. Manual Technique
- A. Impulse of Will   1   2   3

- B. Baton Technique (if applicable)
  1.   Grip   1   2   3
  2.   Right/Left Hand   1   2   3
  3.   Direction Pointed   1   2   3
  4.   Flexibility   1   2   3

- C.   Entrances/Cut-offs
  1.   Preparation   1   2   3
  2.   Tempo   1   2   3
  3.   Dynamics   1   2   3
  4.   Mood/Style   1   2   3

Chapter 8: Kitchen Sink

When guarding against poor vocal technique in your singers, one of the most important tasks you have is to listen, listen, listen. That is the obvious part. The other key is to watch them carefully. To my knowledge, no voice teacher or conductor has yet to be sued for malpractice, but I have no doubt that day is coming. Don't be the one who encourages poor vocal health simply by lack of attention!

What can you do about this? First, you can guard against it by educating your singers on the signals of sickness before it becomes a real problem.

You can do this at the beginning of the year in a communication via e-mail. Most vocal problems result from the following:

1. Short-term upper respiratory illness: cold, flu, sinus, allergies.
2. Gastric issues resulting in reflux
3. Vocal misuse and abuse

The first of these are probably the most prevalent. Your singers need to know when such things are coming on and the difference in the symptoms and remedies. Of course, this is all affected by voice irritants such as pollen, inhaled irritants (pollution), smoke, and chemical fumes, in addition to the actual illnesses they catch from each other, children, or that door knob.

The second, gastric issues, has become much more prevalent since our diets and eating habits have spun out of control. Your singers absolutely need to know that if they are hoarse for more than 2 weeks in a row, they need to search for the cause. If they rule out respiratory issues, they need to ask their physicians about reflux. Reflux can chronically burn their vocal folds while they sleep and they don't even know it.

The third includes a variety of issues. Most of these are ways in which we encourage misuse of the singers through poor vocal technique in our rehearsals and performances. But, this can also be a result of a lack of education on the basics of vocal health outside of rehearsal as well. We too frequently make demands on our singers such as over-singing in large halls or over orchestras, changing temperatures from space to space, etc.

Vocal Health in Rehearsal

1. Listen, listen listen. You are the only one doing that as they sing. Use the entire rehearsal as a laboratory for healthy singing.
2. Encourage your singers to hydrate before coming to rehearsal. It takes at least two hours for your singers to hydrate on the cellular level! It can't be done on the 10-minute drive to rehearsal. Any less hydration is purely topical.
3. Encourage your singers to get plenty of rest around rehearsals and performances. There is nothing like a rested body to help provide a rested voice and mind.
4. Encourage your singers to use good posture during rehearsals. Remind them of what that is. Let them sit, let them stand, let them move around if you have enough room.
5. Teach them to breathe. Never let up on this. Remind them often throughout the rehearsal.
6. Remind them not to abuse their voices by speaking (or singing) too loudly. Also encourage them to keep their speaking voice at a normal pitch that is not too low and to conserve their voices, especially on rehearsal and performance days.

You are obviously not in a position to prescribe medicine for your singers, but you must at least have a cursory understanding of medications and remedies that are on the market, especially those that are over-the-counter and easily accessible to your singers. Perhaps you have a doctor, nurse, or pharmacist in your chorus who can help with this. However you get your information, you need to have it readily available.

We all know that hydration is one of the keys to healthy singing. What you may not know is that it takes about two hours to hydrate from the cellular level. Anything else is topical and does not reach the vocal folds. There is some good information provided in "The Perfect Blend" DVD, as well as some pretty incredible film of my own vocal folds – worth the price, and all geared toward choral singers.

The information on vocal health and health in general is constantly changing. Since "The Perfect Blend" was published, we have welcomed the arrival of Mucinex® on the market, an over-the-counter medication now in generic form.

Mucinex® is a pill form of guaifenesin that was only available with a prescription or over-the-counter syrup. All of these are expectorants that help make the mucous more fluid thereby keeping the fleshy covering of the vocal folds moist.

One of the most important aspects of remaining healthy is keeping the vocal folds moist and clear of too much thick phlegm which may be due to various causes such as illness or pollution. The most healthy way to keep the folds clear is to gargle. Here is just one possible mixture to keep on hand to keep your folds in good shape.

Dr. Gould's Gargle

1/2 tsp. salt
1/2 tsp. baking soda
1/2 tsp. clear corn syrup
6 oz. warm water
Gargle in small sips, 3 x per day.

Vocal Health Questions

When you are approached by singers who say they are sick, the questionnaire below is a good starting point in pinpointing the problem

1. Are you hoarse after singing in rehearsal?
2. Is the discomfort muscular (extrinsic) or on the inside (intrinsic)?
3. Has the hoarseness lasted more than two weeks?
4. Are you hydrated? Do you "pee pale"?
5. Are you getting enough rest?
6. How is your phlegm? Thick, thin, colorful?
7. Are you warming up appropriately before singing?
8. What medications are you taking?
9. Are you abusing your voice (yelling, smoking, Karaoke)?
10. Have you already seen a physician about this? What was the diagnosis?
11. Are you contagious?

Repertoire

As mentioned before, you may begin your first chorus experience without one single piece of music appropriate for that chorus. For those of us who have been around the block, so to speak, we may not remember that really great piece that we sang with that chorus we conducted three jobs back!

There is nothing so useful as keeping a list – or even better, a notebook of all of the songs that you consider your "hits." I call them **Sugar Sticks** – the sweet things that you really want to keep devouring from time to time.

I can't tell you how often I go to my Sugar Sticks notebook. There are separate books for each voicing, my own treasure trove of tried and true. If you don't have such a thing, start it today!

My All-Time Favorites List/Sugar Sticks
All pieces are published by Shawnee Press, Inc.

Title	Composer/Arranger
Lambscapes	Eric Lane Barnes
America, the Beautiful	arr. Marvin Gaspard
Let Me Be the Music	Portia Nelson, David Friedman arr. Anne Albritton
The Awakening	Joseph M. Martin
The Quest Unending	Joseph M. Martin
Variations on "Jingle Bells"	arr. Mark Hayes
Why We Sing	Greg Gilpin
When I Have Sung My Song	Ernest Charles arr. Tim Seelig
Little Star	Jill Gallina
Ave Maria	Charles Gounod arr. Anne Albritton
Music in My Mother's House	J. David Moore arr. Anne Albritton
Swingin' with the Saints	arr. Mark Hayes
Sing for the Cure	Various Composers Komen for the Cure, Breast Cancer Foundation
The Wisdom of Old Turtle	Joseph M. Martin

Merchandising

(Recordings and T-shirts and Coffee Mugs, Oh My!)

Products are very important in "brand awareness" for your chorus. Not only that, doggone it, people like them. Just be careful in deciding what YOU think people want to own and the reality of what they really will purchase and of course, your singers like to have chorus items.

Regardless of what you decide to use to market your chorus – any product at all – the following form is a useful tool. It will help you decide if there is truly a market for what you are proposing and if there is, what your realistic expectations should be.

So, you want to make a commercial recording of your group to sell to the masses. This is a slippery slope. The most important question to ask yourself is "Why?" Just after that is "Who really wants to own this?" If the answer to the first question is "Because we can," it is probably not a very good idea. If the answer to the second question is (truthfully) "Not very many people," then the idea may need to be tabled.

With today's technology, almost everything is recorded – both audio and video. But not to be sold – at least legally. Be very careful before deciding to sell the recordings of your concerts. There are royalties to be paid. If you do not pay them, not only is it unfair and unethical, you will be caught and fined.

Most new conductors (and some old ones) think that they can make a great deal of money from selling recordings of their chorus. After all, they have improved so much in the three months since you took over! Most of those conductors have storage closets or garages full of unsold chorus recordings — right next to the other items that didn't sell in the fund-raisers from past years.

There are a million items out there to purchase. And there are a whole bunch of people who would love to sell them to you. Make sure you have a "focus" group to help you before you purchase too many of anything!

Merchandise Planning Worksheet

Project name

Planned release date

Key appeals of the product

Target market and first-year sales forecast:

     Members

     Family members

     Fans

     Concerts

Sales:

     Internet

     Book stores

     Appearances

Similar product and sales history

Income (first year):

     Sales

     Underwriting/Sponsorship

Expenses:

     Layout/Design of new cover

     Cost of Product

     First-year advertising costs

Cash forecast:

     Expense

     Income (first year)

     First-year net income

Outline marketing plan

Profits go to _____.

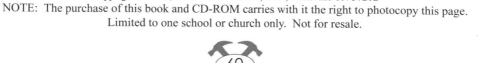

Getting Out of Town

One thing that we must continue to do is to provide exciting "carrots" for our singers. Those can be in the music we sing, the venues we choose or the groups with whom we collaborate.

A major "carrot" we have is the possibility of travel, be it 30 miles or continents away. The benefits of travel with your group cannot be quantified, there are just too many. Not only do you hone your skills when you take a tour outside your own environment, but there is an esprit de corps that is built within the group. Somehow, when we get away from home, everyone likes everyone else in the group (for short periods of time). The discovery of new places, new people, and new concert venues is exciting and bonds the singers together like nothing else we do.

One of the major concert promotion/tour companies with whom I have worked is ACFEA. They sent following travel questionnaire was to help any group decide whether it is ready to travel and what type of travel is available.

I have known groups that simply use travel as an incentive to keep singers involved, rather than quality music, or meaningful outreach. This is not a healthy way to utilize travel – it's like having a baby to save a marriage. Travel should be an outgrowth of a successful program, and considered very carefully.

Travel Questionnaire

1. The fundamental question: Why go on tour? Unless you have clear goals for the tour you cannot achieve all that is possible. Spend a LOT of time on this.
2. Is your group ready to tour? A major project like a tour can be very beneficial to an ensemble, but it can have negative effects as well. What makes you think you're ready?
3. Depending on whether your tour objectives are musical, cultural or philanthropic (or a combination of those), where in the world should you go?
4. What can your members afford? What can you raise? Therefore, what is your budget?
5. What repertoire makes your group sound best? Can you perform it well with the people you expect to participate in the tour? Can you perform it well to appreciative audiences in the places you want to visit? What accompaniment do you need?
6. What staff resources do you already have (administrative and financial) to handle the work of the tour? What extra resources will you need, and will they be volunteers? If not, how will you recompense them (salary, free or partially free trip)?
7. Bearing in mind that there is no such thing as a "free trip." How many people will actually travel at no cost to themselves (conductor, accompanist, etc.), and how will you cover those costs?
8. When do you need to start planning a tour? Think about when you want to tour and work backwards from there to allow time for all that needs to be done. If the answer is less than nine months for anything but the simplest tour for a small group, try again!
9. What are the pros and cons of arranging a tour yourself versus engaging a tour company?
10. How will you choose a tour company if you decide not to arrange the tour yourself?

To Retreat or Not Retreat

In our business, we like to use the word "retreat" as a noun. Often, we would like to use it as a verb, but seldom do we have that luxury. If we were to retreat, there would be no one left to hold down the proverbial fort.

Much like traveling outside your own city, having a choir retreat can be one of the most productive things you can do for your chorus. I have helped facilitate countless retreats in my hundred years as a conductor. A great deal of education is necessary in helping your singers understand the benefits of a retreat and making sure that you have as close to 100 percent participation as possible.

The key word to planning a retreat is BALANCE! No one wants to spend an entire weekend of their lives just rehearsing. While we as conductors can't imagine anything more fun than that, most of our singers think we have lost our minds. If they are going to devote an entire weekend to the process of learning their music, they want to have some fun along the way.

In the same vein, your singers do not want to spend an entire weekend at a choir retreat and do nothing but play. If they are going to take an entire weekend out of their lives, it probably is not going to be with you! Sorry, that may sound harsh, but it's true. The key word to planning a retreat is BALANCE. Yes, I know I've already said that.

We used to have what we lovingly called "Lock-ins." We gathered on a Friday evening and were "locked in" the gymna-cafetorium until the same time the next day. Thank goodness that trend is gone — at least for adults. It was not productive for singing, to say the least. Of course, the Turtle Creek Chorale does hold the Guinness Book of World Records for the longest choral concert in history, singing for over 20 hours straight!

If you can manage a retreat that lasts from Friday evening at 7:00 p.m. until Sunday at noon, you have 41 hours to plan. Subtract 16 hours for two good eight-hour nights of sleep. Then subtract time for meals and other physical necessities and you're down to about 18 hours of rehearsals and activities that you actually need to plan.

From there, you begin to work your magic by filling your singers' time with productive rehearsals, bonding exercises, and just plain fun. I would never agree to any weekend retreat that didn't include 12 hours of good rehearsal time. Once again, just as in planning one rehearsal or one concert, you must plan very, very carefully in order for it to be successful.

The singers need to be given a schedule such as the one below. You, on the other hand, will have the entire weekend planned on the 5-minute schedule in order to keep it moving and productive.

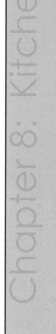

Retreat Schedule (Sample)

Friday:
Afternoon: arrive at location, check in, etc.
7:00-10:00 p.m. Full Chorus Rehearsal
      8:30   Break
      9:00   Choreography
10:00   Social, team building or "family" activity
                Rest, relax, prepare for Saturday!

Saturday:
8:30-10:00 a.m. Full Chorus Rehearsal
      8:30   Warm-ups
      9:30   Subgroup break-outs
10:00   Break
10:15-12:00   Full Chorus Rehearsal

12:00-1:00 p.m. Women sectionals/Men – lunch
1:00-2:00   Men sectionals/Women - lunch
2:00–5:30   Full Chorus rehearsal
3:15   Short break
3:30   Run full concert – from memory
5:30   Break
7:00   Dinner and Entertainment (faux talent show!)

Sunday:
9:00-11:30 a.m. Rehearsal
11:30   Share time/bonding
12:00 p.m.   Depart for home

Other possibilities:
Leadership building
Memorial or history of the group
Theme retreat with costumes, etc.

Job Performance Evaluation

This is not something we particularly like or anticipate eagerly. However, it has been my experience that in the long run, it is an absolutely necessary evil. There have been times in my own career when I was not given a yearly evaluation and the saying comes to mind, "no good can come from that."

In our profession, the most difficult thing about evaluations is accepting who is doing the evaluating and what their qualifications are to be making judgments about your job performance. In most cases, the people making those decisions about our job performance have little or no expertise with which to perform that function.

In this situation, the tool they use is crucial. Your input into the process and the final result is also important. You may think it is unnecessary to spend much time on this. One day, however, you may be surprised when someone enters your professional life who really places a great deal of importance on evaluations. Not only that, evaluations can be an insurance policy for you. When someone gets a "bee in their bonnet," good, annual job evaluations can be invaluable to you. On the other hand, bad evaluations can serve as handwriting on the wall and encourage you to update your resumé (which we will talk about later).

If your supervisor is not a musician, it might be worthwhile to include one or two other people in the evaluation process who might have first-hand knowledge of what you actually do. On the other hand, do whatever you can to make sure you are not being evaluated by 10 or 20 people who sit on a governing body over your organization. Indeed, "no good can come from that." Also, never be afraid to refute something in your evaluation if you feel it is unfair or unsubstantiated.

The following tool is one that I think is broad enough to be used effectively for most situations.

Employee Performance Evaluation

Employee Name:	Job Title:
Period Covered:	Reviewer:

Description of Major Duties

Explanation of Ratings

1 – Outstanding	4 – Needs Improvement
2 – Excellent	5 – Unacceptable
3 - Acceptable	

Knowledge	Employee has a thorough understanding of appropriate processes and procedures involved in effectively performing assigned tasks.	Rating:
Comments:		

Skills	Employee possesses technical knowledge needed to efficiently and effectively perform assigned tasks. Employee uses technology in an optimal manner.	Rating:
Comments:		

Communication	Employee communicates adequately, effectively, and constructively in written and spoken language using technical resources appropriately. Employee keeps management and co-workers updated on issues and conditions.	Rating:
Comments:		

Teamwork	Employee works well with other employee[s] [exh]ibits willingness to assist coworkers, accepts efforts to integrate work, and ac[cepts] [...] from peers.	Rating:
Comments:		

Resumé/Bio

Two documents need to be kept updated at all times: a bio and a resumé (more like a CV or "curriculum vitae," meaning "course of life").

The first is your professional bio that you send to people when you do a guest conducting gig or workshop or for inclusion in a program. We are normally not too bad at keeping the simple bio updated as we use that one more often. It goes in our own programs and we send it around when we do guest appearances, etc. In my teaching, my students are required to keep an up-to-date bio because they are constantly auditioning for jobs – both singing and conducting.

The other more involved resumé is what we don't keep up with. This is your "Job Hunting" tool (just in case you find yourself looking around a little). There are many tools available to help you keep your resumé updated. The bio that you send to people when you are making an appearance needs to be in paragraph form so the "presenter" can simply cut and paste it into their program. Most often, they do not have or take the time to write it for you if you send only the long resumé.

My bio in this book can serve as a sample of the one that would be included in programs. It is easy for the presenter to edit and written much like a press release or a news story; the most important information first and becoming less important with each subsequent paragraph.

On the other hand, when you are seeking a job change or someone actually asks for a resumé, it is not in paragraph form, but organized in specific areas for easy reference pertaining to the things in which they are interested (see the following sample).

Both are important to keep updated on your computer. You never know when an opportunity will arise when you need to shoot off a bio or a resumé. The bio needs to be one page. The resumé can be as long as you need it to be!

RESUMÉ (Sample)

NAME

CONTACT INFORMATION
> Don't make them search for this – they want to hire you!

EDUCATION
> Include degrees and other educational experiences.

EXPERIENCE
> Who has paid you money for what you do, i.e., jobs?
> Start with the most recent and work down.

CONDUCTING EXPERIENCE
> There are many ways to do this, depending on what is most
> impressive in your resumé. Start with the most recent.

ADDITIONAL EXPERIENCE
> Internships, Apprenticeships, Assistantships, etc.
> Workshops, Clinics, etc.

PRINCIPAL TEACHERS/CONDUCTORS
> List the ones people might recognize or the ones who
> made an impact on you (quantity is not the key).

SUCCESS IN RUNNING CHORAL PROGRAMS
> This can include participation numbers, budgets, etc.

ACTIVITIES/HONORS/AWARDS
> Many people like to know you are well-rounded in today's world

ADDITIONAL CREDENTIALS
> If you have certifications, etc.

REVIEWS
> Add credible reviews here (not the one from your Mother).

PERSONAL INFORMATION
> You may include personal information such as marital status,
> children, etc. Employers are not allowed to ask.

Chapter 9: Lists

Some of the information in this book does not call for actual forms or questionnaires, but it is nonetheless important.

In this chapter, some things that are educational and entertaining that I have used throughout my years are included. Some of the lists are serious and full of information; some I have kept for my own amusement; some I put on my door or bulletin board from time to time; and some are suitable to share via e-mail with colleagues.

An entire folder on my computer (that I will not include in this book) contains the fun and silly e-mails that people have sent me through the years. These are taken every time we go on retreat and portions are shared throughout the weekend just to spice things up. You know, the ones like "Children's Book Titles That Never Got Published," or "You Know You're a Redneck When…."

Those will be included in the next book – and most likely have to be self-published!

Additional Lists and "Stuff"

What I Learned (from my colleagues)
Getting to Know You
I Didn't Practice Because...
Beatitudes
Seelig-isms
Emotional Line
Risk
12-Step Program
FUNdraisers

Chapter 10: Vocal Resources
Aural Modeling

What sound is in your mind's ear? Do you have a favorite choral recording? Do you even listen to choral music? (You don't have to answer that aloud.) However, whatever you listen to consistently helps set your tonal preferences for your own chorus. You know it when you hear it; you just may not know how to get there.

Your chorus will only sing as beautifully as you can imagine them singing and only as beautifully as you are able to translate that imagined tone to them via the choral technique you are teaching them. But first comes that aural ideal of yours. There are obviously choral techniques you admire and some you avoid (or should).

Consider the aural modeling your singers have had in their experience: Britney Spears, Randy Travis, and Jessica Simpson. We may pine for the good old days when we had Frank Sinatra, Peggy Lee, or Perry Como. But we also had Johnny Cash and Ethel Merman. Regardless of your opinion of the new pop/classical crossovers, thank goodness the public at least gets to hear what we would call a more "legit" sound. Do you play your favorite choral groups for your singers? Can you describe for them why you like the sound (and how you hope to achieve it with them)?

If they never hear anyone "better" than themselves, they are striving toward a nonexistent goal housed only in your head.

You need to have your five favorite recordings at your fingertips should someone ask you what you like. It can be a single piece or an excerpt from a larger work. Put them in one place where you can listen to them consecutively. What is it that draws you to each? Is there a common thread? Does that tell you something about what you are striving for in your work with your choruses? You absolutely should play these for your chorus. Now, just for fun, compile a CD with your five least favorite choral moments just for yourself! Don't put the names or groups on it just in case someone finds it.

Choral Warm-ups

If you are having trouble with any aspect of the actual music your choir is making, look first at your warm-up routine. Everywhere I go, I find that choral musicians are desperate for help in warming up their choruses and keeping them fresh. Here is my suggestion:

Make five separate lists and put them on your computer. Name them something like:

1. Posture
2. Breathing
3. Phonation
4. Resonance/Articulation
5. Blend

As much as you may hate to do it, you need to look at some of those old, tattered, and worn-out exercises and let them go. Just as with the old clothes in the back of your closet, you may not remember where you got them, may wonder why you ever liked them, and certainly know that half of them don't fit anymore. Your warm-ups need sorting through. If you don't know why you do a warm-up, and if it does not have a specific goal you wish to achieve, put it in a garbage bag and send it on its way. Then, every time you make a rehearsal plan, choose at least one exercise from each group to begin the rehearsal. Always do them in order.

The order above not only takes you from the large muscle groups to the small, but it also begins with the individual singer and moves toward the group. By beginning with movement, exercise, stretching, etc., you help your singers leave their "baggage" at the door. They will be ready to go.

So, the following pages are just a beginning for those lists you are going to make. Through the years, as you learn new "tricks of the trade," simply add them to the appropriate group. When you find yourself falling into a rut, go back and switch them out in your rehearsal plan. You'll never be boring again.

The following lists of warm-ups may look strange to you. Hopefully, they do not. If so, please refer to "The Perfect Blend" book and/or DVD for explanations.

Posture

Each time you meet with your chorus, you simply must begin with at least one exercise dealing with posture or alignment. Not only do singers need to focus on how to hold their instrument, but by allowing them to move, stretch, bend, etc., you are getting their blood flowing. Start with the large muscle groups and work down from there. Not only will it help get their bodies involved, it will help them leave their "baggage" at the door and encourage them to focus on you and the task at hand.

Some Posture Exercises:

> Sternum Power
> Morning Routine
> Massage
> Karate Kid
> Faux Jog
> Wiggle Jog
> Faux Sit-Up
> Windmills
> Bend and Stretch
> Pat Down
> Hug Yourself
> Row Your Boat
> Raggedy Ann/Andy
> Dive Up and In

Add your own:

Breathing

There is never too much attention paid to breathing. Never stop reminding them that they need to breathe. We don't breathe efficiently or sufficiently in our daily lives — perhaps only 20 percent of our vital capacity (lung volume). Once a week, we need them to kick that up a notch, or two — to 70 percent or so! Select exercises that increase capacity as well as help the singers understand their entire breathing mechanism.

Breathing Exercises

> Three Balloons
> Sternum Power
> Farinelli
> Prep Breath
> Air Elevator
> Inner Tube
> Italian Breath
> Dog Breath (Panting)
> Savings Plan
> Fountain of Youth
> Sit and Learn
> Collapse and Connect
> Swimming Breath
> A Rose Is a Rose

Add your own:

Phonation

Be very careful when adding vocal fold participation into the mix. Know that your singers have not warmed up, or have not had the time to hydrate. Help them by being conscious of easy onset of the tone — floating on a steady column of air. Unless your chorus and singers suffer from breathy, inefficient tone quality, encourage them to use the breath to carry the tone to their listeners.

Phonation Exercises

> Bumble Bee
> Blow Your Finger
> The Scream
> Bowling Ball to Feather
> Inner Tube ABCs (breath pacing)
> Hummers – with Air
> Show Me the Octave
> Inner Tube Octave
> Bowling Octave
> Buckets of Cement
> Personal Neck Brace
> NASCAR
> Messa di Voce Magic
> Boo-Boo
> Alleluia
> Floating Down
> Siren

Add your own:

Resonance/Articulation

Only when the first three "food groups" of warm-ups have been addressed can you or should you move on to the actual sound your singers are making. With the bodies engaged, instrument held appropriately, breathing mechanism ready to go, and free vocal fold participation, are you ready to start tweaking the actual sound through resonance adjustment? Our task is to teach our singers as wide and varied a vocal tone vocabulary as possible. In this way, we are able to communicate to them quickly and simply what kind of sound is required for each type of repertoire we perform.

Resonance/Articulation Exercises

> Woofers and Tweeters
> The Three Bears
> This is a Fah-fah-fine Day Today
> Get Rid of the Nose
> Playing with the Palate
> Nose Fun
> Get the Floor Out of the Way
> Baby Bird or Swan?
> Elastic Band
> Look Ma, One Hand
> Fish Lips or Horse Teeth?
> Matching Vowels
> 2-Finger Ah
> 1-Finger Oh
> Meow

Add your own:

Choral Blend

Everyone has his or her own idea of what the illusive "blend" entails. When I am asked what my definition of "blend" is, I say it starts with a comprehensive understanding of posture! Then, the next issue is breathing — making sure everyone in the ensemble is breathing with the same mechanism. Of course the next important factor is freedom of the vocal fold vibration. If you have some singing breathy (hypofunctional) and some singing tight (hyperfunctional), there will never be blend. Matching vowels and matching resonator adjustment come next. And finally, when all of that is under control, we get to play!

Blend Exercises

    Yawn and Sigh
    Choral Pyramid
    Matched Pearls
    Final Note
    Beauty Box
    Path to Legato
    Tractor Pull
    Spin Cycle
    Pulsating Legato
    Bella Signora
    Vowel Migration
    The "Bad" Vowel
    Keeping Space in Pianissimo
    Finger Cymbals
    Heart Tactus

Add your own:

Chapter 11: Additional Resources

As mentioned earlier, most people could never imagine what it really takes for us to do our job well. Some of that may be our own fault for making it look so effortless! This book is filled with resources to help make the tasks easier, but there are still a few more. However, they are ever-changing as they include resources that are altered many times during each year that passes.

Some, of course, remain forever. Others come and go. For example, almost as quickly as a list of web sites is formulated, others crop up. And some simply pass on into cyberspace. New recordings are made, replacing our favorites, or adding to them. Following are some resources for you to maintain on your computer that you can constantly update as the years come and go.

Books
The Perfect Blend and The Perfect Rehearsal by Timothy Seelig
Shawnee Press, Inc.

Conducting Choral Music by Robert L. Garretson
Prentice Hall

Directing the Choral Music Program by Kenneth Phillips
Oxford University Press

The Choral Singer's Survival Guide by Tony Thornton
Vocal Planet

DVDs
The Perfect Blend and The Perfect Rehearsal by Timothy Seelig
Shawnee Press, Inc.

Websites
www.shawneepress.com
www.choralquest.com
www.choralnet.org
www.acdaonline.org
www.chorusamerica.org
www.galachoruses.org
www.menc.org
www.nats.org
www.ifcm.net

Author's Bio

Educator, speaker, leader, singer, conductor, motivator, writer, guide, friend, parent.

As an educator, Dr. Seelig holds four degrees, including Doctor of Musical Arts from the University of North Texas and the Diploma in Lieder and Oratorio from the Mozarteum in Salzburg, Austria. He was the Artistic Director for the world-renowned Turtle Creek Chorale (TCC) for 20 years and has been on the adjunct music faculty at the Meadows School for the Arts at Southern Methodist University since 1996.

Dr. Seelig's early training was as a singer. He made his European operatic debut at the Staatsoper in St. Gallen, Switzerland and his solo recital debut at Carnegie Hall in 1991. Two solo recordings, EVERYTHING POSSIBLE and TWO WORLDS have been released and he is a published arranger, lyricist, and writer.

After stepping down from the TCC, Dr. Seelig became the Director of Art for Peace & Justice, a program of the national nonprofit Hope for Peace & Justice (www.H4PJ.org). He will continue the work he started with the TCC by using the arts to raise awareness and further social issues and causes. In addition, he has been named the Artistic Director in Residence for GALA Choruses, Inc. and continues his teaching at SMU.

Dr. Seelig continues a busy guest conducting schedule with workshop appearances throughout the U.S., Canada, and Europe. As a clinician, appearances include state and regional conventions of the American Choral Directors Association and state, regional, and national conventions of MENC. He has conducted all-state and honors choirs, including South Dakota, Connecticut, Michigan, New Mexico, Florida, and Oregon. He serves as the Chairman of the Choral Advisory Committee for Dallas Independent School District. Prestigious universities such as Michigan State University, Kansas University, Texas State University, Stetson University, and Vandercook College have invited him to lecture.

During his tenure with the TCC, it grew from 40 to 350 performing members in six separate ensembles. The $69,000 budget increased to $1.7 million annually. Under his direction, the Turtle Creek Chorale recorded 36 compact discs, reaching the top 10 on the Billboard classical charts. The chorale has been the topic of two PBS documentaries, the first of which was awarded an Emmy in 1994.

Invitations have been received to perform at eight national, regional, and state ACDA conventions and the Eastern Regional MENC convention. The chorale has performed across the U.S., including Carnegie Hall four times, and in Barcelona, Prague, and Berlin.

Dr. Seelig has been honored on many occasions. A few of these include University of North Texas Distinguished Alumnus, The Dallas Historical Society designation of "history maker of today," and the Dallas Theater Center's "pillar of the Dallas artistic community," as well as carrying the Olympic torch as a community hero. Most
recently, Dr. Seelig was awarded the Hero of Hope award for his 20 years of service with the TCC.

He is the proud father of two incredible, and thankfully grown, children. No grandchildren – yet!

Reviews

"A good rehearsal begins with a good warm-up and no one explains all the ins and outs better than Timothy Seelig.'
The VOICE of Chorus America

"The Perfect Blend is a hands-on book that never becomes tedious or overwhelming to read. Seelig's humorous and holistic approach to technique makes this book not only a joy to read, but more importantly, reminds us that we are, after all, teaching the person inside the singer."
AMERICAN MUSIC TEACHER

"Dr. Seelig takes eclecticism to new heights."
GRAMMY MAGAZINE

"Conductor Seelig has raised this group up from the ranks of amateur choir to one receiving wide attention for its excellent performances of appealing, fresh repertoire."
FANFARE MAGAZINE

"As fine a male chorus as I'll ever hope to hear."
AMERICAN RECORD GUIDE

"An accomplished chorale, under Dr. Timothy Seelig, theirs is a joyful noise."
USA TODAY

"Known as a fine singer, he also slices a thick cut of ham."
FORT WORTH STAR TELEGRAM